FOLKLORE METHODOLOGY

Publications of the American Folklore Society
Bibliographical and Special Series
General Editor, Wm. Hugh Jansen
Volume 21   1971

Folklore Methodology

FORMULATED BY Julius Krohn AND
EXPANDED BY NORDIC RESEARCHERS

by Kaarle Krohn

TRANSLATED BY Roger L. Welsch

PUBLISHED FOR THE *American Folklore Society* BY
THE UNIVERSITY OF TEXAS PRESS, AUSTIN & LONDON

International Standard Book Number 0-292-70092-X
Library of Congress Catalog Card Number 76-145448
© 1971 by the American Folklore Society
All Rights Reserved
Type set by G&S Typesetters, Austin
Printed by The University of Texas Printing Division, Austin
Bound by Universal Bookbindery, Inc., San Antonio

Originally published in 1926 in German as
Die folkloristische Arbeitsmethode by
The Institute for Comparative Research in
Human Culture, Oslo, Norway

Gratefully dedicated to the immortal
remembrance of
Moltke Moe, Axel Olrik, and Antti Aarne

Foreword

This book is based on lectures that Professor Krohn gave in Oslo during the winter of 1924–1925 and later revised for publication. It is the first systematic attempt to state a method of studying folkloristic materials. For centuries men had collected folkloristic texts and had commented on them. They had discussed such matters as connections with local customs or religious beliefs and stylistic details, but they had not tried to formulate a method of investigating folklore. Professor Krohn did not seek to study the psychological background of folklore, to describe folklore as a student of literature might wish him to do, or to compare it with sociological and anthropological data. Such worthy enterprises were far from his mind. He was suggesting a method of investigation which he thought was likely to clarify the circumstances of the origin and dissemination of a folkloristic text. His critics have not clearly perceived this limitation of what he was trying to do. Nor have they fully realized that he thought the folkloristic method, as he called it, just as suitable for the investigation of proverbs, riddles, superstitions, and other folkloristic materials as for the study of narratives in verse and prose.

The development of the folkloristic method, with its frequent but erroneous later restriction in the popular mind to folk narratives, began in Finland. It differs from other methods of investigation in that it requires a considerable number of texts as a basis. Such large numbers were easily available in Finland, where Elias Lönnrot and many collectors after him had gathered them for the study of the narrative songs in the *Kalevala*.[1] Editors of the Homeric epics and collectors of traditional ballads and tales had assembled what they could find in the fields in which they were interested, but they did not seriously endeavor to invent a method of studying what they had gathered. Svend H. Grundtvig and Francis James Child corresponded about the editing of a collection of ballads, but their exchange of ideas did not lead either of them to put together a simple statement of the task or to discuss the nature and contents of the historico-critical headnotes that they were writing for their collections.

The Finns naturally regarded the folksongs that Lönnrot had used for the basis of the *Kalevala* as very precious objects of literary and critical study and recognized their value as tradition. Professor Julius Krohn, the father of Professor Kaarle Krohn, undertook to investigate these songs in the latter half of the nineteenth century. He was aware in a general way of other investigations of traditional materials but recognized that the Finnish texts were peculiar in their abundance and their history. Texts could still be easily gathered—the last traditional singer was still living in the first half of this century—and the origin of some songs in western Finland was apparent, although the tradition was living only in eastern Finland and especially in Karelia. In a very obvious way this body of material suggested problems of the place of origin and the manner of transmission. Unfortunately Professor Julius Krohn, who tragically was drowned during a vacation on the Gulf of Finland, did not complete his study of these songs. He had however encouraged his son Kaarle to collect Finnish folktales and to write a dissertation on northern animal tales. These tasks prepared him for writing this book, but other circumstances, such as the

[1] For additional comment see my "Precursors of the Finnish Method of Folklore Study," *Modern Philology*, 25 (1927–1928), 481–491.

organization of his own collections, his dissertation, and the editing
of his father's manuscripts, occupied him completely for a large
part of his life.

One of Professor Kaarle Krohn's favorite students, Antti Aarne
(1867–1925), undertook to use the folkloristic method in studying Märchen much as his teacher had used it in studying animal
tales. After he had completed his dissertation, Aarne catalogued
the tales in the archives of the Finnish Literary Society in FF
Communications 3 and 5 (1910, 1911) and wrote an exposition
of the method he had used in his dissertation, FF Communications
13 (1913). This was, I believe, the first work of its kind. He continued with various catalogues of Finnish and other tales, a note-
worthy concordance of the major national collections of tales, FF
Communications 10 (1912) that he left incomplete, and various
monographs dealing with individual tales. It is particularly important to note that he published three volumes of studies in
riddles, FF Communications 26–28 (1918–1920). As Professor
Kaarle Krohn told me in 1925, Aarne chose to write these studies
in order to show that the folkloristic method could be employed in
this genre as well as in narrative genres.

Knowledge of the Finnish method spread slowly and criticism
did not contribute much to its development until Walter Anderson
published a meticulous investigation of a single tale: *Kaiser und*
Abt, FF Communications 42 (1923). This investigation in over
four hundred pages that dealt with more than five hundred versions
was a sensation in the world of folklore and has been criticized
again and again for more than a generation. Professor Krohn did
not utilize Anderson's work in his lectures. It contained a statement of method with some improvement over Aarne's version in
details as well as an exhaustive history of the origin and dissemination of a tale. In 1931 Professor Krohn reviewed studies in folk
narratives that employed the folkloristic method in FF Communications 96. It was in many ways a sort of leavetaking. We need only
to read this book of 1925 to perceive that he had found the

method generally useful in folkloristic studies. In the search for information about where and when a tale was invented and how it was disseminated, the folkloristic method is invaluable and this book remains an admirable exposition of the method. Today we have gone further in folklore studies and are asking questions that the folkloristic method never tried to answer.

ARCHER TAYLOR

Translator's Acknowledgments

I am grateful to Professor William H. Jansen, who put my translation into English and whose sense of humor is obviously unshakeable. I would also like to offer thanks to Dr. Richard Dorson, who first suggested Krohn's work to me for translation, and Roger Abrahams, who encouraged me to submit my translation to the American Folklore Society's Bibliographic and Special Series.

Preface

The Norwegian Institute for Comparative Culture Research honored me with a commission to give lectures dealing with folklore methodology for its first session in 1924, and I attempted to describe the experience of Finnish researchers in a half century of work of thousands of compatriots. Of interest are not only their fortunate finds and auspicious efforts but also their mistakes and failures. The latter have encouraged renewed, ever more penetrating, research, especially in the area of the *Kalevala* cycle.

It was not possible within the restricted format of the lectures to give the various problems equitable and satisfactory treatment. In a young science it is above all important to point out the difficulties that should gradually succumb to the common effort of future researchers. It has been with the intention of arousing such an interest that questions have been posed that defy the solution of any one all-encompassing answer.

In preparing this book for publication, I added as the first chapter a discussion of Julius Krohn, the founder of methodological folklore research in Finland, to clarify the conditions under which the "Finnish method" was developed.

At this time I wish to express the thanks I owe my father for the good fortune of having him introduce to me the wonders of

Finnish folk literature, in the beautiful language of the Finns—
my own language from childhood on.

I proclaimed my indebtedness to my deceased friends, Moltke
Moe, Axel Olrik, and Antti Aarne, by the dedication of this study.

Finally, sincere thanks are due Professors Walter Anderson,
Knut Liestøl, Gustav Schmidt, and Archer Taylor for their kind
examination of the manuscript.

K.K.

Contents

FOLKLORE METHODOLOGY

I. Julius Krohn

THE EMINENT KALEVALA SCHOLAR Julius Leopold Krohn was born in the Finnish city of Viborg (Swedish: Wiborg; Finnish: Viipuri) on May 19, 1835, the very year that the earliest edition of the *Kalevala* appeared. His paternal grandfather, a German, had emigrated from Rügen to Petersberg, and his father, Leopold Krohn, had come to the vicinity of Viborg to an estate inherited from his father-in-law. This other grandfather was also a German and had married the daughter of a Finnish clergyman. At home both of his daughters, including Julius Krohn's mother, received a German upbringing.

Mrs. Julie Krohn, nee Dannenberg, who could speak the language of the people from her youth on, was interested in public education. When the Krohns had moved into Viborg for the winter so that their children could attend school, she organized in her home a public school for girls, for whom no educational institution existed at the time. Her linguistic ability later helped her to follow the literary efforts of her first-born, efforts which were financially supported by both parents throughout his lifetime.[1]

Julius Krohn's mother introduced him to the elementary levels of knowledge in the German language. He received additional instruction from a Russian student and a French student in their native tongues. Although his parents planned to send him to a German school in Petersberg at the age of eleven, his frail physical constitution and his mother's dependence on him did not permit it. Thus he was turned over to his mother's brother, a reader at the Swedish Gymnasium in Viborg, for two years of instruction in Swedish.

When Krohn entered the Gymnasium in 1848, the nationalist movement inspired by Snellman had reached its zenith. During this year Runeberg published the war memoirs of Ensign Stål, with the national hymn as its introduction, and in the following year Lönnrot published the new edition of the *Kalevala*. Finnish nationalism was at its strongest in Viborg, where the three languages of the upper classes—Swedish, German, and Russian—stood in contrast with lower-class Finnish, the regional *koine*.

In Viborg lived Jaako Juteini, a municipal official and the first poet of autonomous Finland. He aroused rural Finland with his very popular song, "We Too Deserve Respect." Also in Viborg, from 1845 to 1847, the pioneer Finnish author Pietari Hannikainen published the first public newsletter in Finnish. It was to appeal to both educated and uneducated Finns. In 1845 a branch of

---

[1] The author gratefully records that his grandmother's financial support permitted his first collecting trip to the oft-praised country of the Archangel-Karelian rune singers and taletellers.

the Finnish Literary Society at Helsinki was established in Viborg.

The pupils of the Gymnasium clearly reflected the nationalistic efforts in which their teachers were playing an active part. They produced three or four handwritten newspapers and they even attempted to establish a literary society. Among the Swedish texts of their literary exercises pop up occasional Finnish poems. It is reported that there were direct demands at the school for cultivation of the Finnish language.

As a result of this nationalistic activity, Krohn began to turn his interests to the study of Finnish. He was the only one in his class who really worked at Finnish school assignments; the others had greater practical ability with the language and could squeeze through with little effort. He read more from the *Kalevala* than the course demanded, and he attempted to compile an index of obscure words in the work. Krohn was assisted in his translation by his maternal aunt, Amalie Fabritius, who told him much about the beauty of her North Karelian homeland and the noble character of its self-reliant farmers. In the summer of 1853, after the school term, he took a trip into this area with the family of his maternal uncle and discovered that reality exceeded even his expectations. From Punkaharju, frequently visited even today by tourists, Krohn wrote, "Here, my dear parents, I must remain silent, for this cannot be described—only felt. It was with pride that I carved into the beech, where one is supposed to record his name and nationality, that I am a Finn."

In Helsinki, where Krohn continued his studies, Swedish was totally dominant except for the lowest level, which consisted of workers who had immigrated from the countryside. It was the most unfavorable time imaginable for efforts toward a Finnish culture. In 1850 an edict was issued banning all literature in Finnish with the exception of religious and agricultural publications. The student organizations at the University, which had allied themselves with the nationalist movement, were dissolved in 1852. Even activities of the Finnish Literary Society at Helsinki were restricted:

it was prohibited from accepting as members women, artisans, farm workers, and, above all, students.

At the wish of his parents, Julius Krohn decided to take up medicine. But by the second semester he had already attended the language exercises of Lönnrot, who had just been installed as a professor of Finnish language and literature. In order to unite his interest in Finnish with his preparations for a medical career, he resolved to translate Stöckhardt's treatise on chemistry into Finnish. Since the Finnish literary language was not yet fully developed, Krohn's mastery of it was not complete and thus he was unable to complete this translation for a full decade.

Soon, however, Krohn's philological interests gained the upper hand. When Snellman took up his chair in philology in 1856, Krohn was among the first in attendance. At the same time he studied history and attempted to translate mentally into Finnish whatever he read. He also practiced translating Latin into Finnish. Similarly, for exercise Krohn translated Finnish folktales into Swedish and after a short time back into Finnish. He spent the summer of 1857 and the winner of 1858–1859 in the provinces of northern Karelia and northern Savo in order to drink from the purest well of the folk idiom. In Helsinki he had no opportunity to speak Finnish, for even the nationalists at the University used primarily Swedish in their affairs. He could regularly converse in Finnish only in special sessions with a school friend from Viborg.

Julius Krohn's progress in his mastery of Finnish can be seen in a letter to his parents, dated March 14, 1855:

As you know, I wrote Finnish essays last spring under Professor Lönnrot; they looked rather colorful after he had corrected them. The previous term he had no time but now he is again accepting my work. Today I brought him my first fruits and just look! There are only a few unimportant errors. Indeed, he told me I should give the essays to the *Suometar* editor so that I can get a start in their newspaper. Just think of such encouragement from a man like that! I felt as if I were blushing all over, because several others were also standing around.

That was a rich reward for the great amount of time and effort I have applied to the task of bringing vitality to the language of my homeland. Oh, now I will work with even more desire and patience, for I see that the goal is attainable. On the other hand, I will not follow his advice to have my essay published—because, with all due respect to his judgment, I still do not view my essay as mature enough to send on its own into the wide world. It will have to sit at home a while and wait until its wings have grown larger.

Two years later he began to prepare for the candidacy examination and he reported in a letter dated March 10, 1857, "Actually, the essays are supposed to be written in Swedish, but it is possible to use another language. As a matter of principle I will use *Finnish*." His candidacy examination was the first at the University to be written in Finnish.

In school Krohn had written down many bits of poetry in German and Swedish. As a student he had decided to cease his literary attempts until he was in a position to take them up in Finnish. His first original poem in Finnish is dated 1856. At the Schiller Festival in 1857 he made his debut with a translation of "The Diver." A few "Tales of the Moon," in the pattern of Andersen, also stem from his student years.

In 1858 Krohn established the first Finnish folk school, in Helsinki, along with eleven other nationalist students; it had to be supported for several years with a voluntary staff and private means. At the same time he gave instruction in Finnish at the Senior Swedish Girls' School—which initially was also gratuitous—and gave private tutoring to a few ladies and students who were interested in Finnish. On October 20, 1860, he replied to his mother, who had expressed concern that his energies were being spread too thin:

Mother, you call the instruction of Finnish youth of our capitol a distracting interest. For me it is one that has grown close to my heart. Every advance of the Finnish people fills me with more joy, as if it were actually my good fortune too. Each setback in this regard strikes the most painful chords in my soul. How could I call this a distracting

interest, this thing that fills such a great part of my thoughts and emo-
tions? I am just put together in that way and you must let me go my
way. I am driven by my instincts just as the migratory bird is driven
again and again from the warm latitudes into the cold and desolate
north. He cannot do otherwise and neither can I.

After his candidature examination in 1860, Krohn spent the
summer on trips to the Finnish interior that had become so beloved
to him, and in the fall he began to work on a dissertation on Finnish poetry, with Finnish culture as the background, about the era
of Swedish domination. After the completion of the treatise he
wrote to his parents, on September 30, 1862:

> Mother, if you will, please translate or summarize for Father what-
> ever parts of this that might be of interest to him. At various times I
> have told you the principal thoughts that dominate the whole work—
> primarily a description and proof of the fact (overlooked until now)
> that during Swedish domination the Finnish people were not without
> national spirit and that the Finnish language was the general colloquial
> tongue at all levels of society even after 1700.
> . . . The certain hope that the discovery of this fact must contribute
> to the establishment and elevation of nationalism thrills me. For it
> shows that Finnish culture is not a figure of the imagination, devised
> only yesterday by Johnny-come-latelies; it is actually a national concept
> that has only been suppressed at various times.

In a later letter, dated November 11, 1862, Krohn reported that
he had delivered the purely historical segment of his dissertation as
a lecture for the benefit of a private Finnish folk school and that
he was also to deliver it in Viborg during the Christmas season.
"Whatever it brings in will be distributed as a subsidy for good
translations into Finnish or an original work in the language. For
precisely such powerful display of Finnish *belles lettres* is now necessary to make Finnish acceptable in the home."

In the same year Julius Krohn was named University Lecturer
in Finnish Literature and Language and he established, with his

wife Emma Nyberg, a purely Finnish home, the second among the educated circles of Finland.

The Nyberg family, as well as the Krohn family, came from Swedish Pomerania but had already been established in Finland for a century. Raised in Helsinki, Emma had not had the opportunity in school to learn even Finnish grammar. Quite early Runeberg's patriotism had aroused in her heart a warm feeling for the Finnish people. As a tutor in the Swedish coastal city of Nykarleby in 1856, she wrote to her elder sister, "I would be so happy if I could in some way participate in the spread of education throughout our country. If I were a man, I would settle down in some Finnish village in the interior in order to get to know these people. The establishment of schools and clearing of the wilderness would be my life's work. He is fortunate who has here a beautiful land to love, but three times fortunate is he who can accomplish something useful for his country."

Personal love helped her overcome her linguistic difficulties; with a dictionary in her hand she deciphered the letters of her fiancé. In the first year of their marriage, Krohn spoke only Finnish while his bride always answered in Swedish, but by the time their eldest son was born Emma spoke only Finnish—with the single exception of counting the laundry, which was done with Swedish numbers, so much more familiar to her.

In order to give the children a Finnish education, the parents were prepared to have the mother move away from Helsinki with them during the school term, for the only school of higher education in this city that used the Finnish language had been forcibly removed to a distant country village. The establishment of a private Gymnasium from resources gathered throughout the country saved the family from this disruption. Finnish educational institutions, several of which had to be supported by means of voluntary contributions, and the development of a Finnish-language theater, as well as other national cultural efforts, demanded significant economic support.

Devoted labor was also continually demanded; even the nature of one's work could not be determined by personal wishes but was instead decided by the demands of the movement. In order to accustom intellectuals to material written in Finnish, Krohn published the first illustrated Finnish periodicals in the years from 1864 to 1866 and from 1873 to 1880. To this same end he translated half a dozen of Walter Scott's novels into Finnish. For school youth he wrote tales based on Finland's history, which were derived from his own research. Krohn was also thinking of small children—especially his own—when he translated Andersen's tales into Finnish and published five illustrated books of beautiful little poems. For the ecclesiastic use of the people, he worked with a committee on a revision of the Finnish hymnal. He promoted national literature and the literary language with a few thin volumes of his own poems; of special note is the "Emma Cycle," written as a memorial to his first wife, who had died early.

In 1876 Krohn married the principal of an upper-level girls' school in Helsinki, Minna Lindroos. She too was from Helsinki and had learned Finnish only after she had finished her formal education—in part by comparing the Finnish Bible with the Swedish one. She had founded the private school with her sister and her brother-in-law, B. F. Godenhjelm, teacher of German at the University.

Krohn contributed to the scientific study of Finnish by assisting in the preparation of a grammar on Finnish syntax and by writing an Estonian grammar from a Finnish point of view for use by the University.

He was, however, primarily interested in literary history; even before the completion of his dissertation he had published an essay dealing with recent rural poetry. In 1866 his anthology of Finnish poetry appeared, which also contained biographic notes. In the winter of 1874–1875 he lectured on Finnish literature in a private women's school. Krohn prepared a complete Finnish literary history, which he lectured on at the University, where he had become a full professor in 1885. The history was published after his death. Krohn had already touched on medieval poetry in his dissertation, and as a professor he dealt with it more extensively in his lectures, which were also revised for publication after his death. His lectures on Finnish mythology, a theme that first attracted his scientific interest in 1869 when he began his study of Finnish history, eventually also received extensive treatment.

In the women's academy mentioned above, Krohn dealt with the primary work of Finnish literature, the *Kalevala*. He completely reworked his esthetic commentary for the fiftieth anniversary of the Finnish Literary Society in 1881; later, in 1892, a German translation of the commentary appeared in Veckenstedt's *Zeitschrift für Volkskunde*. At the same time he compiled, as a basis for a genetic investigation of Kalevala songs, a survey of the diverse song variants in Finnish as well as Estonian linguistic areas, including analogous themes and motifs among adjacent peoples. In his exacting search for corresponding materials he was led even further afield, as he described in the letter he wrote to his parents on February 26, 1881:

Occasionally I begin to tire. As I have told you, I did not think that I would find anything belonging to the Kalevala among the East Finns. Everything that was known about the matter suggested this conclusion. But you can't trust the experts. Right away I found such interesting things that I had to study carefully this people's folk literature, scattered throughout a mass of Russian periodicals and Hungarian works. More than two months have already been spent on this and there is not a chance that I will finish it in yet two more months. Besides the fact that I can read Hungarian only very slowly where precision is demanded, a few days ago a situation came up that at first struck me as calamitous. In Savvaitov's Zyrian grammar I found approximately thirty pages of songs and stories that I absolutely had to read, in order to see if anything of interest to me might be in them. But the good man had printed them *only in the original language*. So there I stood like a duck in a thunderstorm. In Friedrichshamn (Swedish: Fredrikshamn, Finnish: Hamina) there is supposed to be a Professor Aminoff, who understands Zyrian quite well, but now, during the school term, the sickly man would need a good deal of time to work out a translation for me. What else could I do? Thursday forenoon I read through the grammar and today I have just finished my thirty pages. Finnish, Hungarian, and Russian were the three levers that helped me lift that beam so quickly. And in passing the obstacle I learned another language.

I almost forgot to tell you that I also studied Tartar songs and tales, in which Radlaoff and Schifner were gracious enough to spare me the learning of that language, too. They did cost me some effort, however, for it was a matter of five large octavo volumes—500 to 800 pages each. But the effort had its rewards in that it now permits me to trace certain parts of the *Kalevala* as far distant as the Altaic region. I wonder what will come from such research in the long run and the broad view. It's like a laborious climb in the mountains: all at once, in one moment, the struggle and agony disappears. Now I am undertaking the final edition of comparisons with Russian and Germanic heroic lays, old friends from the past summer and fall that will quickly flow from my pen.

In spite of all his efforts to complete this work, whose section on esthetics had already won the Finnish Literary Society's Jubilee prize late that summer, the end seemed to lie somewhere in the uncertain future. Krohn reported of his "beloved but sometimes difficult labor" to his parents on August 18, 1881: "During the many rainy days here [at a vacation resort] I have worked on a new section and unfortunately noticed that it is not coming along as easily as I had thought and hoped it would. On my return to Helsinki I will have to go through the manuscripts of all the variants again—which will take perhaps three weeks. I have found, you see, that my annotation and excerpts are not sufficient. Therefore during this current stay I cannot complete the two selections I had planned on, but rather can only prepare them."

In the fall his ability to work failed and it was over two years before he regained his full powers. During this enforced leisure, however, new concepts that led to a total revision of Julius Krohn's work methods were quietly maturing.

First, Krohn became convinced that one dare not proceed, in comparisons, from the form of the song that was preserved in the *Kalevala*. A thorough investigation of the manuscript song transcriptions that had been meticulously preserved and enlarged through later collections of Lönnrot had completely shaken his faith in the reliability of the printed text as evidence. He found that not all characteristics of the *Kalevala* appeared in the same contexts among singers and—with no exceptions—that they were not once to be encountered in traditional folk variants.

Even more important was the insight that by no means could every variation of a Finnish song theme be contrasted with a comparable foreign analogue but rather only the original form of such a song theme. In arranging variants of one and the same song, Krohn found that the variants were geographically defined and stood in geographic relationship to one another. In a letter to the Hungarian linguist P. Hunfalvy, dated October 16, 1884, Krohn explained that the distinctive character of his new methodology involved "arranging and observing various versions chronologically and topographically before I draw final conclusions; for I have found that only in this way can one separate the original components from later additions."

Julius Krohn's genetic interpretation of the *Kalevala* appeared in two parts in the years 1884 and 1885. He prepared an edition for Swedish translation that combined a survey of the material and an investigation of individual songs; it was not published until 1891. At the same time some of his essays, translated into German, were published as condensations in Veckenstedt's *Zeitschrift für Volkskunde*, for consumption by a wider audience. At the conclusion of these essays he spoke of the results of his research:

As can be concluded from the discussions above, the songs of the *Kalevala* are certainly, in terms of the general nature of their components, by far not so ancient as has been believed up to now. Similarly, it has been indicated here, even if only by suggestion, that an important part—indeed, even the major part—of the material has been borrowed from myths and legends of other peoples. Especially this last assertion has doubtless aroused painful feelings on all sides, since there has been such a desire to view the *Kalevala* as a thoroughly indigenous product of Finnish folk culture. On the other hand, it can also be seen that this will offer new nourishment for those who believe that the intellectual capabilities of the Finnish people are less than those that have been observed often among more civilized and highly developed peoples. Something similar seems to have been feared by Castrén, too, when he first discovered large amounts of Scandinavian borrowings in our epic. "Perhaps," he said, "it does not lie in the interest of Finnish nationalism that this thought be expressed; yet the spirit of science demands that the situation eventually be brought to light. Nothing would please me more than if the opinion which I am about to discuss here were refuted by a just critic." This whole fear is actually without foundation. For even if the Finns have borrowed the greatest part of the substance of their epic poetry from afar, they have done only what all other peoples have appeared to do more or less throughout all time. Nor can I find anything at all degrading in this. Of course the thought would be grand that one's own people had been in a position to create from the depths of their own soul everything that then determines its pride and joy. But even more inspiring yet is the aspect of one great culture stream, which, having its source under the palms in India and on the fertile plains of Egypt, turns its powerful current toward the West, enriching southern Europe, only to turn again to the East, along the way enriching northern Europe. One people after another accepts it, develops beneath its influence, and then sends it on to its neighbor— enlarged and improved. It is senseless to bicker about the greater or lesser creative abilities of one or another people; this is simply a question of time. The peoples who are, as a result of their geographic location, influenced at a later time by the culture stream naturally must participate in development at a later time and therefore appear less blessed with originality because the inheritance passed on to them is all the greater. But nothing keeps them from subsequently becoming through their own efforts greater than their predecessors. In regard to

the literatures with which we are here primarily concerned, it is after
all not the material per se that is most valuable but rather its artistic
transformation. Schiller found the material for his *William Tell* ready-
made, as did Shakespeare for his *King Lear*. But upon them they then
impressed the stamp of their intellect, and the dramas cited are now
their works and no one else's. The same is true of the *Kalevala*: even
if the substance has been borrowed in large part from neighbors, it has
been nonetheless so independently recast, has attained such an individual Finnish character, and—last but not least—it has arrived at such a
humanly valid, refined poetical form that the Finnish people can with
pride call this epic their own—a work that in beauty stands second
only to the immortal masterpieces of the Greeks, a work that has however risen far above any poetry that can be created by the folk.

Omitted from the above is a personal expression regarding
Castrén's words that Krohn addressed to his Finnish compatriots:
"Castrén is quite right when he puts the demands of science first.
One cannot build on deception and lies, even for the advantage or
honor of one's own nation. If the admission that the major part of
the material in the *Kalevala* was borrowed from the outside world
deprives the Finnish nation of the honor of this immortal creation
then it would be our duty nonetheless to make that admission, no
matter how bitter that might be for us."

Doubt in the absolute originality of a national work has always
been received with great discomfort in the minds of a people. As a
result of this, Krohn's work was no longer accepted with complete
enthusiasm. In addition, he did not concur with the view expressed
by A. A. Borenius (Lähteenkorva) that the songs of the *Kalevala*
did not originate at the locale where they were most abundant, in
Archangel Karelia, but had instead migrated from Finland. Borenius sought their origin in part in West Finland, in part in Estonia.
The East Finns viewed this as an embezzlement of a possession
entrusted to them by tradition. In defense of this possession,
August Ahlqvist, Professor of Finnish Language and Literature,
published a polemic about the Karelian nature of the *Kalevala* that

was based on the printed text of the new and occasionally the old editions, but without the slightest consideration of the underlying variant manuscript materials that had been collected at a later date.

The valuable and enduring part of Krohn's work, however, does not rest in its immediate results. In his comparisons with similar motifs in the literatures of other peoples, he had not attempted to compile merely correspondences that would in his opinion prove some particular, actual connection. Instead, he also sought out those relationships which he was obliged to discard, so that other researchers would also have an opportunity to use these. He also included a good deal of analogous material that he encountered in Finnish magic charms. Similarly, his conception of the actual mythic content of both genres gave way to a more realistic view, according to which the original runes were of legendary content, the heroic songs of historic content.

The real importance lies in Krohn's geographic methodology that contributed heavily to the attainment of subsequent results and continued to be influential for some time. It was applied in the area of animal tales even during his own lifetime by his eldest son. The usefulness of this method has also been validated in other areas of traditional transmission.

Among the first to affirm its value was Gaston Paris in his discussion of *Le roman de Renart*,[2] where he called it "a new and rigorous scientific methodology." He added, "In addition to the fact that it is based on the division of tales into types, which other scholars have already done, it is basically geographic in the sense that it attempts to delimit the areas in which the tales are formed, propagated, and modified." He described the procedure as "ingenious and in particular cases very reliable." Krohn did not, however, live to see this and other acknowledgments.

That the geographic method of research arose in Finland can be explained by the uncommon wealth and variety of song mate-

[2] *Journal des Savants* (1894–1895).

rials available there for the researcher. To be sure, previous Finnish song collections lacked proper notation of the site of collection, which is so necessary for the geographic technique. These had to be established through a precise investigation of manuscripts, procurement of new transcriptions from the same area, and, above all, comparison of geographically documented variants with undocumented ones. Julius Krohn applied a good deal of time and effort to this difficult work, especially in the preparation of the planned edition of old epic songs. The first volume of *Kalevala* variants was already in print when death overtook him in a sailing accident on August 28, 1888.

The folklore methodology of Julius Krohn was expanded by Nordic research in practice as well as theory. Ample expositions of this are offered in various areas of folkloristic tradition, such as the following:

Antti Aarne, "Wie die Rätsel untersucht werden sollen," Chapter One of *Vergleichende Rätselforschungen*, I, FF Communications No. 26 (Helsinki, 1918).

Antti Aarne, *Leitfaden der vergleichende Märchenforschung*, FF Communications No. 13 (Hamina, 1913).

Kaarle Krohn, "Kalevalankysymyksiä" (Kalevala Problems), I, *Journal de la Société Finno-ougrienne*, XXXV (1918).

Axel Olrik, *Nogle Grundsaetninger for Sagnforskning*, Danmarks Folkeminder, No. 23 (Copenhagen, 1921).

II. Demarcation of the Field of Work

THE PRESENTATION of a methodology presupposes a delimiting of the field of the work in which the methodology is to be employed. A scientific field should enclose a homogeneous area in which any particular segment can be worked by one and the same fieldworker with consistent scientific coverage. Esthetics, for example, is, as the theoretic explication of beauty, a unified discipline. In practice, however, efforts within this relatively young science have been long divided because of the heterogeneous divisions necessary for the disciplines of literature, creative arts, and music.

Today researchers no longer consider themselves capable of significant accomplishment in all of these areas.

As a result of the principle of consistent effort, not only have more materials been accumulated and their individual details penetrated, but also specialization within scientific disciplines has progressed. An exception to this general tendency would be the widening of the scope of folklore research according to Arnold van Gennep's new handbook.[1]

The scope that I am here assigning to folklore is wider than that accepted by the early traditionalists, who viewed only stories, legends, songs, beliefs and customs, witchcraft, etc., as "transmitted by tradition." The progress of our science has forced us to add the study of all rituals, games and dances, popular saints' cults, the home and village, kitchen utensils, all kinds of tools, minor and major arts, institutions created by the people or surviving from ancient periods, and, finally, types of emotion and expression that differentiate the "popular" from the "sophisticated."

In the English *Handbook of Folklore* (1914) by Charles S. Burne, the scope of folklore is still restricted to the spiritual culture of the people and expressly excludes technical culture: "In short it covers everything which makes part of the mental equipment of the folk as distinguished from their technical skill [*sic*]."

To what extent spiritual or aesthetic culture and material or technological culture can be joined within one and the same scientific activity must seriously be questioned. And mere quantitative bases are not the only consideration in this discussion. As C. W. von Sydow has stated, the two areas place totally different demands on the ability and methods of the researcher.[2]

The ethnographer must possess a sense for form and color, a comprehensive knowledge of the commodities and their manufacture, as well as a certain, practical ability to determine types and technical details

[1] *Le Folklore* (Paris, 1924), p. 30.
[2] *Våra folkminnen* (Lund, 1919), pp. 18–20.

of various objects. The research area of the folklorist is completely different: it involves the thought-world of the people, the transactions of the people—insofar as they have developed from native concepts as well as folk literature and not from purely technical points of view. There are also totally different auxiliary sciences demanded for the various areas of study. While folklore research is associated above all with literature and the history of religion, philology, and psychology, ethnography stands allied with archaeology, art history, the technical sciences, et al.

In addition, folk music must be set up as a special field apart from spiritual culture. It demands special skills and training of its collectors and students. An ear for music can no more be expected of a folklorist than an eye for external form. His interests must be directed primarily toward the inner world of thought, and his powers of observation will be taxed quite sufficiently by this.

If we separate from folklore, in its widest sense, material ethnography on one hand and folk music on the other, we are left with the areas of folk belief and folk literature. Should these also be separated?

We find traditional superstition associated with certain material objects, natural phenomena as well as cultural products. The cultural products, which for the most part were produced because of specific needs, were only later employed for superstitious purposes. The connection of folk belief with the material aspects of folk culture is too restricted and superficial to justify its separation from nonmaterial folk literature.

The impossibility of distinguishing between areas of folk belief and folk literature in scientific investigation was expressed again by von Sydow:

All folk literature, and especially the folk legend, is usually more or less shot through with superstitious images. Therefore it is not possible to investigate Märchen or legends successfully without a knowledge of the superstitious concepts that are present in the content and characteristics of these tales. It is equally true that folk belief and custom cannot be satisfactorily studied without reference to the Märchen and legend; for this literature is an ancient inheritance that can transmit to us superstitious attitudes and customs as a living practice in an older, more original form.

Instruction in a superstitious skill and a legend about the application of the same are found together. In descriptions of superstitious customs, magic incantations often appear that have to be considered folk literature. A separation of these two in the collecting or the ordering of a collection is totally impractical. Finnish magic sayings are, moreover, so entwined with epic songs of the same metre that in the Archives of the Finnish Literary Society all songs, magic sayings, and superstitious customs had to be numbered in one series (b), while nothing seemed to stand in the way of individual categories for Märchen and legends (a), proverbs (c), and riddles (d).

To be sure, folk literature offers invaluable material for linguistic research and also for literary history. Before, when the language and literature of a people were bound together as one academic subject, their folk literature was also included. Nowadays, usually only the most ancient literature remains as a specialized subject of linguistic research because of its generally standardized interpretation. Folk literature, too, continually excites the interest of linguists because of the obsolete words and idioms that it preserves. A phonetically trained linguist can make important contributions to the explanation of mythological names and concepts associated with them, but a talent to detect the formulaic in language is neither sufficient nor essential for the investigation of the thought content of folk literature.

The literary historian stands very near the folklorist, for he frequently finds a need to seek the traditional source of some literary phenomenon. His material, sophisticated or art literature, demands, however, a particular, learned feeling for esthetic composition and performance. Although an understanding of the simpler constructs and forms is sufficient for the folklorist, he needs above all the ability and practice that enable him to draw the basic, essential characteristics and expressions from a mass of variations.

The gradual realization of the emergence of folklore as an academic discipline, separate from linguistics and literature, can be seen most clearly in the ever-changing designation for the academic chair that was developed for Moltke Moe at the University of Kristiania (Oslo) in 1886. Initially his professorship included Norwegian folk speech with, as a minor subject, Norwegian folk tradition. In 1899 it was changed to a chair for Norwegian folk tradition, including medieval literature. Today it is dedicated exclusively to the science of Norwegian folk tradition.

In the Scandinavian terms for folk tradition or "folk memory" (Norwegian: *folkminne*; Danish: *folkminde*; Swedish: *folkminne*), we find united the meanings of the English words "folklore" and "folk knowledge," and of the French term *tradition populaire*. "Folk memory" excludes, on the one hand, the nontraditional, ephemeral knowledge of the people and, on the other, the nonspiritual heritage of the people. But even these restrictions are not sufficient.

At the universities of Helsingfors and Dorpat an older term was retained for the official title of the professorial chair: "folk poesy" (Finnish: *kansanrunous*; Estonian: *rahvaluule*). The word "poesy" —understood in its widest sense—contains an essential complement to the concept of traditional knowledge. The functional scope of folklore research does not encompass all traditions maintained in the folk mind, but rather only those that are poetically colored, fancifully rewritten, or purely invented. In the differentiation between folklore and the other areas of research that draw on traditional material, the essential factor is the presence of an artistically creative element.

Folk belief belongs to the field of folklore insofar as it contains that which is called superstition, such as weather omens—for example, those concerning Siebenschläfer day (June 27) and the following seven weeks. A prediction based on true experience interests the folklorist only insofar as it, like the proverb, has attained a crystallized form.

While the theological scholar seeks the true content, or at least the actual psychological bases, of the transcendental concepts of the various peoples, the folklorist turns his attention to the imaginative play of folk fantasy in the development of these concepts.

Similarly, the superstitious segments of folk custom also belong to the realm of folklore. The sociologist finds his greatest meaning in the discovery of the practical and the appropriate in the customs of various peoples; the folklorist, on the other hand, is interested primarily in the overlapping of the folk fantasy into everyday life. Festival customs with their miming performances and plays that present matter very appropriate for folklore research—even when the spiritual content is conveyed not in words but in gestures—particularly encourage free expression of the esthetic drive.

We must establish the same requisites for linguistic tradition. The research of the meaning of individual words belongs in folklore only to the degree that it points to a superstitious concept or that its development reflects an influence of folk fantasy. The folklorist is concerned with the external changes of words only when they do not correspond to usual linguistic laws but instead are explainable in terms of influence of stem rhyme or end rhyme or folk etymology. The distortion of names, particularly in folk literature, falls outside the boundaries of phonetically predictable variation. Among the beings evoked by Finnish magical incantations we find names whose original form and meaning can be determined through comparison of variations in various written sources where their functions are also mentioned, and through the uncovering of similarly sounding names in the indexes of Catholic saints who have similar functions (FFC No. 53, pp. 85–86).

In the same way the folklorist must in his work with idioms determine to what degree their content or form is the result of folk fantasy. The true proverb, as well as the true riddle, frequently contains a concept that gives color and life to the linguistic expression of the idea. In the riddle the idea must be guessed. In the proverb, too, this thought may be omitted or subtle, but it may also be expressed in a postscript.

We find the first, figurative part of Solomon's proverb "like a dog that returns to his vomit is a fool that repeats his folly" (Proverbs 26:11), in the New Testament (Peter II, 2:22). Among the Finns, too, this same proverbial image occurs alone, "the dog eats his vomit again," as well as with its postscript, "the evil man his word." The single-strophe, lyric folk poem is closely related to the bipartite proverb. A four-line Finnish rune song with didactic content is difficult to distinguish from a proverb cloaked in rune form.

All events, including everyday experiences, which are preserved in the folk memory are of little significance to folklore. Of course, a selection of memorable occurrences has impressed the folk. But the work of folk fantasy begins with assigning causal relationships, logical groupings, and internal motivations to these occurrences. In time the actual facts are re-formed to fit the demands of clarity and unity. Finally, images of fantasy are appended. With the aid of historical documents Knut Liestøl has described this development in familial traditions of Norwegian peasants.

The metrically bound form of an item in folk tradition presupposes in itself the certain influence of fantasy. Rhythm and rhyme are of consequence not only in the selection of words; content also has to yield to the demands of poetic composition. All folk literature in metrical form falls within the province of folklore research so long as it is actually traditional.

The "folk" nature of an item as a basic requisite for recognizing any tradition as folklore has been pursued in various directions.

Conception in the mind and subsequent oral diffusion has been contrasted to literary composition and typographic dissemination. This differentiation is unsatisfactory, however, since an art poem can be created without a pen in hand and any transcription can be orally broadcast by the folk.

The contrast between the literarily educated upper class and the common folk has likewise been brought forward. Poetry still alive today in the mind of a lower, folk class was nonetheless fostered in ancient times by the upper classes, too. Even the fact that an important part of our folk literature originated among the socially elevated when oral tradition was also dominant among those people changes nothing of the "folk" nature of such products. On the other hand, Finnish rural poesy that has arisen in modern times is not folklore, although it has made use of ancient rune metrics and was developed before the acquisition of reading and writing skills created well-read and intellectually curious peasants.

The concept "folk" has also been described as "collective" as opposed to "individual." In any case, it is a misconception to seek the collective in artistic creations. Of course, we find antiphony, especially in insult poems, that calls for simultaneous, artistic creation by several people. The single-strophe lyric can be improvised and recited in this same way—one singer alternating with another. But any unified composition, large or small, presupposes an individual composer. In his study "The German Proverb," Fr. Seiler correctly recognized the role of the collective mass: "In the creation of a proverb, just as in the fashioning of a single word or expression, the folk exercise not a creative but rather a selective function."[3]

If folk poetry is consequently the creation of individuals, what then causes it to be characteristic of the folk? Perhaps that the poet is anonymous? The statement of the composer's name is certainly characteristic of sophisticated literature. But surely not every piece of literature whose author is unknown to the performer and his audience is folklore. Folk poetry itself must be unaware of its creator. Even in the egomorphic stage of a folk poem, the ego

[3] *Das deutsche Sprichwort* (Strassburg, 1918), p. 8.

appears as a collective subject with which any performer can identify himself.

The essence of folklore disappears with the development of contemplation. This can be seen in linguistic execution, in sentence construction, and especially in the use of conjunctions.

Folklore, however, is defined not only by external form but also by the inner structure. Folk concepts are often found in literary adaptations. Insofar as these represent for us anonymous, traditional versions, the folklorist must also take them into account.

We can also recognize the degree to which a bit of tradition is folklore by its psychological conception. In folk literature man himself does not stand in contrast to his natural environment, nor does his fantasy stand in contrast to actual experience. Human thought, emotion, and desire, even in their linguistic expressions, can be projected into all the characters and objects of nature; in this way spiritual reciprocity attains an absolute sway in all events: that which is possible in thought also becomes so in reality.

The scope of research for the folklorist consequently embraces folk knowledge when it is (1) *traditional*, (2) *reworked by fantasy*, and (3) *truly folk*. An even narrower definition of folklore research has recently been suggested by Lewis Spence in *An Introduction to Mythology* (London, 1921, p. 12). He states that it should treat the remnants of primitive concepts and customs among the uneducated or semieducated peoples of civilized nations while the study of yet vital religious forms of primitive peoples should be reserved for mythology. It is thus quite incorrect to speak of the folklore of the savage tribes in Africa, America, and Australia. It must be noted that superstitious customs among more elevated peoples are practiced precisely because the belief in their power lives on. There exists however another difference in the folk materials between cultured peoples and primitive tribes, if it is not a simple matter of borrowing from the latter by the former. Axel Olrik (*Gruntsætninger*, p. 33) and Knut Liestøl (*Maag og Minne*, 1919, p. 151) set great store in the definite, structured form of tradition. In this regard the traditions of all European peoples are on a higher level than those of the natives in newly discovered parts of the world. Since, however, the former originally grew out of a similarly vague and amorphous tradition, the exclusion of the latter, insofar as they have been reworked by folk fantasy, is no more necessary than it is justified.

III. Choice and Scope of the Problem

THE FIRST DEMAND that is placed before the folklorist in his field of research is the choice and scope of his problem. Of course it is advantageous to explore a broad perimeter before undertaking a restriction of that area. Various themes are often related and intertwined to such an extent that it would scarcely be possible to treat the components of one theme without an intimate knowledge of several others. A far too rigid restriction in searching for necessary material carries with it the risk of having to repeat the whole, painstaking examination just for some ignored details. But the theme itself, which should be treated from every possible angle, must be precisely defined.

The folklore dissertation of Erik Rudbäck (birthplace: Salme-lainen), publisher of Finnish folktales *Om Finnarnes Folkdikt i obunden berättande form* (1857), dealt with Finnish folk liter-ature in unrhymed narrative form in its totality. According to J. R. Aspelin, the founder of Finnish archeology, it seemed to the next generation of folklorists that, in regard to a similar treatment of other such areas of folklore, this work had exhausted all themes for further academic treatment!

Thirty years later, when I was working on my dissertation, I gathered materials for a general study of the Finnish animal Märchen but I was soon obliged to restrict this work to the tale of the fox and finally had to be content with the adventures of the fox and the bear (wolf). Similarly, Oskar Hackman assembled variants of all of the tales about the stupid ogre for an academic dissertation, but in the end he had to restrict his work to those tales connected with the Polyphemus legend.

Antti Aarne's doctoral treatise embraced three related Märchen, corresponding in part to von Sydow's two. Reidar Th. Christiansen, Lutz Mackensen, and Ernst Philippson each chose a single Märchen type for the same reason. Walter Anderson's *The Emperor and the Abbot* shows how diverse and far-reaching the investigation of one short anecdote can be.

To be sure, one must ask whether the study of even one com-plete folktale does not form an all-too-broad or complex task. K. Spiess said:

Comparative folktale research would stand before a completely unre-solvable task and would have to forego, a priori, establishing and comprehensively ordering the common elements of the folktale among various peoples and studying its related characteristics if that research proceeded from the basis of all available folktale narratives. The inter-woven, intersecting warp and woof would knot into a jumble that sim-ply could not be unraveled. . . . The folktale as a whole is too variable in its design to serve as an object for comparison; in addition, the fact that the relationship is often restricted to completely isolated characteristics indicates that those characteristics lead, so to speak, an independent existence, detaching themselves with relative ease from one context and, with equal ease, entering into another. They are firmly outlined, have a well-delineated size, and are of a material content that can be characterized with a few words. Therefore, they are manageable enough to be used for comparison studies.[1]

Spiess's terminology corresponds to his concept of available Märchen narratives.

Motifs or individual traits can, if they enter into a close relationship with others and appear repeatedly in the same sequence, be assigned to a larger unit that is called a *tale formula*. In Cinderella the motif of the stepdaughter who must perform household duties is bound with that of the envious stepsisters into the *formula* of the mistreated stepchild. The same formula confronts us in the tale of *Frau Holle*. A number of formulas bound together by corresponding and interchangeable features are called a *tale type*. In this rubric are found all of those Märchen that are most closely related. Only the factual content, the nucleus (Pointe) of the narrative can determine the designation of type and classification of individual tales. All tales that tell of an evil stepmother who persecutes the stepdaughter would consequently belong to the Cinderella type.[2]

However, are tales actually so unstable that they cannot serve as the foundation for comparative research? We know that one and the same tale is told in countless variations. Is the relationship between these variants restricted to isolated motifs, or is it not, so to speak, the entire framework of the tale that we recognize with all its variations?

In the Märchen it is quite obvious that the very same motif can occur in different contexts. Dare we infer from this that all narrative tales handed down to us are pieced together from a selection of available motifs according to some arbitrary discretion?

As an example of a motif that commonly occurs in various re-

[1] *Das deutsche Volksmärchen* (Leipzig, 1917), pp. 46, 37.
[2] *Ibid.*, pp. 39–43.

lationships in a large number of Märchen prototype patterns, G. Landtman has cited the motif of the Soul of a Demon in an Egg.[3] This motif was examined more closely in the folklore seminar at Helsinki, and it was determined that it originally was related to the motif of the thankful animals that help the hero seize the egg as booty. The fact that it also occurs more or less incidentally in other complexes is due to the influence of the motif framework discussed above.

In contrast to this hypothesis, it could be posited that every Märchen prototype has its own special motifs. Since Märchen certainly did not all come into being at the same time, however, a later structure may use in its new framework a motif that has already been used elsewhere. As a working hypothesis, at any rate, the assumption that virtually every motif originally belonged to some one particular prototype from which it has migrated, through borrowing, to others is quite justified.

The term "type" has also been applied to this formal Märchen structure even though it has a more general meaning in colloquial speech.

For the principal divisions of Märchen structure, as Aarne simply calls it, the term "formula" (*Formel*) can be applied only with difficulty since this term is usually employed as a contrast to improvisations (e.g., magic formula). The term "episode" is recommended. An "episode" that can also occur as a prototype itself shall be designated as a "wonder tale."

As a rule, the major divisions break into several smaller divisions, which, for lack of a better term, can be called "factors" (*momente*). The frequently used term "motif" has a more specialized meaning, denoting the basic or motivating element of the plot. Each small part of a major component contains in turn several *primary* or *foundation* traits that are more precisely characterized by *secondary elements* or *details*.

---

[3] *Finsk Tidskrift*, I (1921), 133.

In the tale about the rich man and his son-in-law, the episode dealing with the failure of the deceptive message forms a principal element. This tale is further divided into (1) the sending of a letter with a command to murder, and (2) the substitution of a letter with a command to marry. The primary characteristics of the first segment are the sender, emissary, contents, and address of the letter; those of the second, the sleep of the emissary, the substitution, the new contents, and the recipient of the message. Among the secondary characteristics belong the station of the sender and substituter, the manner of death, the mode of substitution, and amplifications (the death of an animal for the marriage order).

From Aarne's listing of folktale types we can sense how precisely the content of any Märchen structure can be determined in its basic components from the very onset. His index of thousands of Finnish and Estonian variants shows how the narratives recorded from the mouth of the folk can be apportioned into a limited number of Märchen types. In Bolte and Polivka's annotations to the Grimm Brothers' Märchen, we find, at the most, a few hundred variants throughout the world. Märchen research can consequently proceed without consideration of all extant folk narratives.

No one has questioned the fact that all extant forms of folk literature in meter can be studied. The Finnish rune song is after all less variable than the Märchen because its simple, progressive verse permits the union and integration of songs of all types and contents. But every rune song has from the very beginning its own, particular verses, and every rune verse—with the exception of certain common expressions, as of address and of reply—was composed in one definite context. Naturally, one particular verse per se, or, more precisely, one particular couplet, can be studied by itself. This possibility, however, in no way contradicts the fact that research is constantly and most profitably striving to determine the original form of a song *in toto* in its formal wording.

This last feature is not however a part of Märchen research. Currently the science can devote itself with a greater chance of success to the determination of the framework of one entire Märchen complex than to the explication of one individual characteristic.

In the examination of superstitious customs, too, it is advantageous to proceed from a comprehensive description of generalizations to a specific goal. The individual characteristics of a magic cure can be as manifold as those of a Märchen narrative, and in their equally numerous variations they offer the researcher sufficient material to which he can restrict himself.

In toothache cures it is worthwhile to define precisely the instrument used to expel the ailment as well as the places where the instrument is allowed to appear and where it is forbidden. In addition, attention must be paid to the time of the magic operation as well as the circumstances of the event. Over one hundred Finnish transcriptions of such cures have been analytically investigated by A. Valve and compared with corresponding Germanic superstitious customs. (Finnish. Verhandlungen der zahnärztlichen Gesellschaft IX [Helsinki, 1912])

The *toothpick*, or other instrument for probing, may consist of:

1. A splinter from a living tree, usually mountain ash, or from a tree struck by lightning. (Since the mountain ash occurs in Finnish mythology as the wife of the god of thunder and is also related to him in Germanic mythology, the same power prevails in both types of toothpick.)

2. The splinter of an object used for a funeral, especially a coffin or cross.

3. A sharp metal object, such as nail or needle, that has been in contact with a corpse, that is, in a shroud or coffin cloth.

4. The sharp parts of the bodies of animals that represent local spirits; for example, the tooth of a water rat or pike, or the tongue of a black woodpecker, in which is hidden the power of a water or wood spirit.

If one is not satisfied with one toothpick (as was the case in sixty-eight instances), magical numbers appear: three (forty-one instances), nine (ten instances), and twenty-seven (one instance).

Even the manner of extracting the wooden splinter is of magical significance: (1) with bare nails or teeth; or (2) with a knife—if possible, a stolen one.

Furthermore, the location, time, and manner of preparation of the toothpick is also of importance. It may be prepared in a kiln, on some special day, during the night, or in secret. It is also important where it is placed in the mouth: in the gums or between the teeth, as well as whether one uses it gently or probes until there is blood.

Similarly, places to which the probing instrument should be taken include:

1. A living tree of a given species.
2. An object of wood.
3. A place between rocks, in the earth, or in water.

The location must be a remote one to prevent further infection. For the same reason the place where the instrument is hidden should be carefully stopped up, and, upon retreating from the hiding place, the concealer is not to look back. Often it is necessary to return the instrument to the place from which it was originally taken.

In the study of riddles it is better to proceed from a riddle formula than from the solutions. In the latter method one obtains a group of riddle formulas that are associated by a common solution. Since, however, the answer common to them is not the only possible one and therefore not always the primary one, but is instead frequently secondary, it unites all too heterogeneous products of the imagination under the same rubric. A grouping based on inner relationships of riddle forms is therefore to be advised if one intends to base his research on a substantial number of riddles that individually offer insufficient criteria. The choice of a group in which the number of items compensates for a paucity of characteristics in each individual one is especially advisable in the study of proverbs as well as riddles.

It goes without saying that a researcher blessed with more comprehensive materials can also accept for study a single proverb or riddle as well as a single superstitious concept or one simple trait of a tale.

The task can be limited geographically or ethnographically, too, in order to permit investigation of variations within a particular area, usually the home area of the researcher where the material is most readily available to him. Projects of this sort are especially appropriate for beginners under experienced guidance.

There are traditions, particularly in metered form, that are encountered only in a single area or in a few closely related or neighboring countries. The Finnish-Estonian variants of rune songs, numbering over 100,000, offer in themselves a strong research collection where the isolated appearance of the material can be checked through comparison with the literature of neighboring peoples.

Even international materials can be available in such massive and disparate forms that the researcher must for the present satisfy himself with investigation of an area in which a relatively intensive collection has been completed. A. V. Rantasalo has in this way compared the superstitious concepts of the Finns and Estonians concerning agriculture with corresponding beliefs among Germanic peoples (FFC Nos. 30–32, 55, 62). The incredible mass of materials had to be offset by ethnographic restrictions. Naturally, in time investigation will be extended to broader areas. The valid conclusions of concentrated work in one narrowly delineated area will always be of greater importance for our science than a frantic dashing about and gleaning of scattered transcriptions from all over the world.

The task of a folklorist therefore must be a well-delineated and precisely defined one. But one must also be careful not to limit too narrowly. The material should at least be assembled within a rather wide radius in order to avoid a repetition of this time-consuming and strenuous labor as a result of insufficient data.

IV. Procurement of Materials

AFTER THE SUBJECT FOR RESEARCH has been established, it is next necessary to assemble as many variants of the same traditional item as possible. Only through comparison of a sufficient number of variants can the accidentally occurring factors in one or several variants be eliminated. Since an absolutely complete collection of transcriptions from several broad areas is virtually impossible, at least one area where intensive work has been conducted and the results of which are available for study should be carefully surveyed. In addition, it must be noted that even when the extant material cannot be obtained in its entirety—even with very diligent effort—some sample of every possible area should be available.

To assemble materials on an international scale would obviously be a very difficult assignment for a single worker. First, he would require bibliographies from every country, in which were listed everything published about folklore, at least in general. The folklore bibliography published by E. Hoffman-Krayer, commissioned by the Union of German Folklore Societies, is a very promising effort in this direction. But even if complete indexes from all over the world, covering even periodicals and newspapers in which folklore items frequently appear, were available, a majority of catalogued publications would remain unavailable to the extent that the folklorist could not use them in his own country and would lack the means and opportunity for extensive travel. This is true to an even greater degree with folklore collections in manuscript form.

Linguistic problems also appear in European materials. The labors of the Eastern European scholar are made easier, not only by the rich variety of folklore materials available to him from East Europe, but also by the knowledge of the several West European languages that he has learned in school. West European scholars have seldom found the time necessary for learning *one* language from the great Slavic family; even with the knowledge of one they would not gain an understanding of the remainder. A further difficulty in the search for relevant materials is posed by the fact that substantial quantities of Western as well as Eastern European texts are transcribed in local dialects. Thus even someone familiar with the written language—unless it is his mother tongue—can decipher the text only with great effort. How much time then remains for one folklorist to concern himself with the smaller linguistic families in Europe, though he may want only to familiarize himself with these languages to the point that he can comprehend contents in general outlines with the help of a dictionary? Command of Finnish as well as Celtic languages, both of which are of great use for a Scandinavian folklorist, has been acquired to date by only one person, Reidar Th. Christiansen.

Non-European materials are currently published in large part in familiar European languages. But it will not be long before the work of native researchers of more progressive countries prevails and manuscript collections accumulate in so many remote corners of the world that trips to all of these places will not be feasible. Even if the quest for materials were restricted to printed, independent publications or manuscripts that are readily accessible— geographically and linguistically—the quantity, which swells annually, decreases the hope that it can be surveyed within any reasonable amount of time. When I was working on my dissertation in the 1880's, this task was still within the realm of possibility— especially since my choice was animal tales, which can be distinguished from other tales at a glance. Reinhold Köhler, at that time the greatest Märchen expert, had the kindness to fill the gaps in my survey. Today a search for variants of a tale prototype form would be a desperate undertaking if Bolte and Polivka's index to the Grimms' Märchen were not at our disposal. This monumental scientific work offers in itself a broad foundation for the comparative study of variants of any tale that appears in the Grimms' collection. Through annotations this index can be expanded. A few catalogs of this sort have been published in Folklore Fellows Communications.

The notes by Bolte and Polivka occasionally contain indexes of variants of individual motifs. In his Jutland dictionary H. F. Feilberg compiled traditional concepts from the Märchen and legends as well as from superstitious customs under applicable key words. A register prepared before his death rests on a far wider literary basis and is scheduled for publication in the Folklore Fellows Communications. However, it too is only a forward thrust toward a colossal effort that, in order to be realized, will require international cooperation and financing.

The future of folklore research depends on an international union like the one planned by the organization of Folklore Fellows in 1907 (FFC No. 4). In accordance, every country would have a local branch where locally printed as well as unprinted folklore material could be preserved and made accessible. Members of the union could for a modest cost secure copies and translations from distant archives through the local administration in their own area.

At least abstracts should be printed from the catalogs of different countries in a more commonly known language; from these, foreign folklorists could see what is and what is not available in various collections. A condensation of such a detailed Norwegian catalog was published in the Folklore Fellows Communications (FFC No. 46).

Finally, the establishment of a general, central library should be considered, where not only books and small manuscripts could be deposited along with offprints and periodicals but also copies of manuscripts from countries around the world.

The most laborious and costly job is still in store for us, however: the publication of all variants of each tradition in a generally known language in the most concise possible form, preserving all significant traits. A study of this kind has been accomplished for the Cinderella tale by Marian Roalfe Cox. Her references are more copious than necessary, however, and they form too thick a tome to encourage emulation.

The correct size of an abstract presumes a style in which all trivial words are omitted, a telegraphic style, and consequent application of abbreviation devices. An attempt in this direction has been made in the publication of Finnish animal tales and a segment of mythic Märchen. Since they were published together in selected, complete texts in Finnish, linguistic problems make them available to foreign scholars only with great effort, while for the Finnish public they represent an uninteresting, sodden mass. We find the variants of the well-known fairytale of the Bremen Musicians in Aarne's study "The Animals in Travel" (FFC No. 11), reworked and translated into German, as well as enlarged with corresponding materials from other countries. The above can serve as samples of how the contents can be abstracted with the greatest possible brevity, at the same time considering all questionable details of these publications. For example, in abstract, Grimms' variant has the following form:

An old donkey that is to be killed flees to Bremen to become a musician. An old hunting dog meets him, as well as a cat, rooster (that is to be butchered for a dinner). In the forest, from a treetop, the rooster sees a light of a robber's house. One after the other they scream before the window. They feast and go to sleep. A robber becomes chief character. The cat (during the lighting of the fire: witch scratching face) on the hearth, dog (bites leg: man with knife) behind the door, donkey (black monster with glowing eyes) on the manure pile, rooster (judge: "bring the rogue here!") on the crossbeam.

This abstract could be abbreviated further, even in modern analytic languages, which are not best adapted for telegraphic style. In ancient Latin this could be condensed even further; unfortunately, knowledge and use of Latin is not at all as common as it used to be. The future will show what a help a literary world-language could be in the diffusion of folklore materials from all languages of the world.

But even if all transcribed material could be brought together from all over the world, it would in many respects still be incomplete, as any scholar in the study of any folk tradition must realize. Especially with non-European variants there is too restricted a number, although there has been a noticeable and earnest effort recently to correct the deficiency. Above all, it would be important to create a systematically organized collection from India, which of course may no longer be viewed as the home of the Märchen but which nonetheless has had an extraordinarily important role in its development. The result would be to obtain an adequate number of variants from each part of a vast inventory instead of relying upon a few minor samples. The Norwegian Institute for Comparative Culture Research has shown a special interest in Indian Märchen in publishing the massive collection of the Norwegian missionary P. O. Bodding, with notes referring to parallels in other Indian collections wherever possible. It is to be hoped that this undertaking will provide motivation for further collection work on Indian soil. Of no less importance would be systematic collection work in Persia—the gateway for all the tales that wandered from India to the Occident—which has been neglected by European folklorists up to now. Work in these countries can only receive its just due when native scholars themselves also realize its importance from a national point of view and broadcast their understanding throughout wide circles.

Without the enthusiastic and unselfish cooperation of over one thousand fellow citizens, 30,000 or even 25,000 Märchen and legend variants could hardly have been assembled. In spite of this vast number of transcriptions, the collection of Finnish materials can in no way be regarded as complete. The gaps that have now and again come to the surface during specialized research cannot be filled in by collectors sent into the field, who within a limited time can cover only a very restricted geographic area, nor by means of occasional contributions by regional collectors. There is still a need for geographically distributed stations in a country where questionnaires or even individual questions can be sent in order to obtain whatever possible explanations, or at least negative evidence, may exist.

In order to accomplish a specialized task, an independent researcher must be to some degree conversant with the traditional literature of the relevant genre. Besides a knowledge of collections made by others, some experience in fieldwork is desirable. A botanist who has concerned himself only with herbariums does not have the same understanding of living nature as he who has plucked flowers with his own hands and come to know them in a fresh condition. The one and a half years that I spent traveling to various parts of my homeland after early vacation trips as a graduate student were basic to my life's work as a scholar.

After publication of my dissertation in the area of animal tales, I felt a great desire to travel through Sweden from the north to the south, or in the opposite direction, in order to obtain a series of variants that could illustrate the development of these tales in actual line of diffusion in the long, narrow country. Since I found neither time nor opportunity to attempt the trip myself, I turned to Swedish scholars, who declared the task unfeasible because of the ever-changing dialects. They were thinking primarily of the difficulties of a phonetically precise transcription of wording in the various dialects that confront the collector in Sweden; they were unprepared for the idea that the confirmation of factual content would be sufficient for the folklorist.

The argument against a continuing, intensive collection project is that it would be difficult to master the constantly changing folklore materials because of not only the cost of preparing copies and translations but also that of preparing the collected masses of variants. These alleged difficulties have been painted in lurid colors by W. Schultz:[1] "If it should continue the way Finns have begun it and folklore societies everywhere have carried it on, in a few years the fool's paradise of Märchen research will be surrounded by such a miles-high mountain range of folklore transcriptions that even American multimillionaires will not be able to work their way through. The chaos that arises presents the greatest difficulties for any processing in terms of general scope and content."

The exaggerated nature of this fear is easily detected if one only considers that the forms of folk tradition even in the investigation of an entire genre can and must be treated as an individual item in terms of their variants. If the researcher has access to a more or less satisfactory collection of folklore books, if he can occasionally visit a rather large library, and if a choice of information sources, such as that planned by the Folklore Fellows, is available to him, then the procurement of variants listed in the index will be neither too difficult nor excessively expensive for any particular study. An investigator should at any rate not be fearful of

[1] *Mitra*, I (1914), 24.

securing a significantly larger number of reliable items of supporting evidence than he needs for his immediate interest, in the event that he has the prospect of an extended field collection.

The greatest difficulty for the folklorist is the pursuit of those documents which lie buried in disorganized collections. Before Antti Aarne's index of approximately ten thousand Estonian Märchen variants was perfected in J. Hurt's collection (FFC No. 25), W. Anderson had to thumb through the whole collection to find five variants for his study of the tale about the emperor and the abbot (FFC No. 42); the sixth variant, however, eluded him despite all his care, and it was only at a later date brought to light by Aarne. At the time when I went through many thousands of song variants in the same collection for my Kalevala studies and had to labor up to eighteen hours a day with Dr. Hurt in Petersberg during my brief Christmas vacation, I certainly did wish every so often during that travail that their number were not so overwhelming. Since then complete indexes, requiring thousands of hours of work, have been prepared for these songs. Participants in the projects of the Finnish folklore seminar can now obtain through this catalog variants of individual songs, from copies written on lone sheets, with a minimum loss of time.

If it is necessary to investigate a rather short song of fifty transcriptions, then the analysis of all the lines, with all their variants, is a task that can be conducted by even the uninitiated in a few weeks during library hours. So it has happened that the same student who was astonished by the need of so many variants has inquired of me, after he had inspected them, whether there might be a few more transcriptions that would clear up some still obscure section of a song.

I am glad to confess that in studying collected variants some few of them will prove to be superfluous because they do not have anything of essential interest in them that has not already occurred in another variant. Every collector can easily discern upon his return from the field and with a closer examination that a certain percentage of his notations are of little or no value at all. During transcription it is not possible to eliminate the less important. Harvesting traditions that are disappearing from the folk consciousness is like harvesting a grain field. No agriculturist strips the grain from the ears in the field; instead he takes it under cover and during the winter, when there is nothing more to harvest, he has time to separate the grain from the straw and chaff by threshing.

A reference to field work in the area of botany is even more appropriate. We find one and the same species of plant in a great variety of specimens in official herbariums, not to mention those in innumerable private collections. Even in one university greenhouse the flora of a single country can be seen in many different forms, frequently arranged geographically. That this has *idem per idem* restricted research would not be seriously suggested by anyone.

The contrary view has of course been expressed that folklore materials are still much too sparse and restricted to serve as a basis for scientific examination. Spiess asserts:[2] "The scholar cannot interview all the hundreds and thousands of people who know a tale; he relies upon the results of his own or others' collecting. Doing this, however, he must always remain aware of the fact that a collection can include only a diminishing, narrow segment of the fairytale inventory actually extant. Thus, the working materials of the Märchen scholar are fragmentary, gleaned by dint of chance."

It has already been admitted that much must yet be done, not only to make available to the folklorist existing materials, but also to increase those materials and to perfect them by means of continued, intensive, and systematic collection.

Denmark provides the best example of the value that copious materials in various folklore areas can have for the science of a country. Through the admirable energy of the private collector Evald Tang Kristensen, Danish materials have not only been ex-

2 *Das deutsche Volksmärchen*, pp. 89–90.

traordinarily enriched but have also been made available in print. Even the variant clusters published in one place by him offer the researcher an effortless opportunity to sort the essential parts of the tradition in question from the fortuitous. Since folk education, with its leveling influence, has made its greatest strides in Denmark, it should yet be possible to conduct this same eleventh-hour gleaning process in other countries.

Of course, the lack of materials for Märchen research in the future remains an inherent difficulty. The time is no longer far distant when literary education now current at higher levels of society will also have penetrated all levels, and traditional knowledge will be displaced. The yet primitive peoples have a choice between acceptance of a higher culture or extinction. The great social movements of our time accelerate the very rapid disappearance of all traditional concepts. Whatever is not now saved and preserved for science will be lost to human knowledge forever. Some methods of folk transmission—for example, the epic cycles of many countries—have dwindled already to a few shreds that survive in the folk memory. Must we then stand back from research temporarily, as well as be without hope for the future?

The question of whether fragmentary materials hinder folklore research from attaining the methodological heights of philology and other older sciences is handled by Axel Olrik with the following rhetorical questions:[3] "Don't well-established sciences work with incomplete materials? Is it after all a distinguishing characteristic of research that the material must be complete or nearly so? Rather, shouldn't it be the *methodology* that makes an investigation scientific or unscientific, that certain method of procedure that recognizes this incompleteness and so provides means for the researcher to overcome it? This method has trained the folklorist to work, not with two or twenty variants of a theme, but rather with two hundred."

3 *Grundsaetninger*, pp. 142–143.

V. Screening the Materials

As SOON AS the greatest possible amount of material has been assembled, it must be critically sorted. The more or less artistically styled samples must first be sorted from the transcriptions of purely oral folklore items. Of course these stylized forms frequently have great value for genetic investigation because of their age. But also because of this merit it is advised that literary variants be treated as a special category.

Literary documents whose folk origins are clearly preserved, as well as folklore that survives in copies, prints, translations, or further reworkings of older documents, are, as such, worthless for the folklorist. If the folklore transcriptions that provided the foundation for the compilation of the *Kalevala* had not existed in a virtually complete form, research on this work of epic poetry—as well as many others—would have had to rely on literary versions in publications of the past and present. What renders the *Kalevala* texts superfluous, quite beyond the genetic investigation of the epic folksong, is the fidelity and conscientiousness with which Lönnrot preserved original collected annotations and even rough drafts of his editorial work. Knowledge of the latter as well as of printed texts can nonetheless be of use in separating oral variants dependent on them.

It is a well-known, if insufficiently observed, fact that a literary version can return to folklore. A secondary literary version sometimes exerts on oral transmission an incomparably more powerful influence than its primary source. Especially significant in this regard are the small newspapers, printed for the people, that replace oral transmission and thus hasten the disappearance of oral tradition from the folk mind.

A piece of folk tradition that reaches the people through literature can migrate orally and undergo change. Such cases, in which the initial model is at hand, are of some interest for the methodological study of folk alteration. Now and then a hybrid form occurs in which it is extremely difficult to sort the literary aspect from the folk aspect. For lack of more genuine evidence this hybrid form may serve, but it must by all means be checked with great care and must be segregated temporarily; for example, in a study of the folk variants of the Polyphemus legend the possible literary influence of Homer's version, as Hackman has demonstrated,[1] must be carefully considered.

Furthermore, the folklorist has to be on his guard against alteration and falsification in material that is ostensibly folklore. He can disregard the tendency of a transcriber to embellish his notation. It

[1] *Die Polyphemsage in der Volksüberlieferung* (Helsinki, 1904), pp. 183–184.

is a more serious situation, however, when two or more transcriptions have been spliced together to fill in various gaps. Most dangerous are additions by the transcriber, inspired by his learning or fantasy. In a few Caucasian legends of fettered giants, a bowel-gnawing vulture that appears obviously points to the literary influence of the ancient Grecian legend of Prometheus. The feuilleton style of one of the variants suggests that this trait originated in the mind of an educated recorder.[2] Even more notable is a report, reputedly folkloric, about the wars of the Circassians and the Goths that corresponds to original, fifth-century accounts and that has thus provided ostensible support for the hypothesis of migration of Caucasian legends to the Far North by the Goths.[3]

The principle of questioning everything cannot be impressed too deeply on the young science that already has its share of problems related to unreliable materials. At least it should be strongly urged that suspect items be treated separately.

An incautious collector can even project his own knowledge into the informant's mouth through ill-composed questions. If one tries, for example, to extract proverbs with the help of a printed collection, then a weary informant may give him an automatic, groundless yes or no answer to the question, despite whether he is familiar with this or that proverb. Similarly, a pressing search for mythological names can bring about the stealthy insertion of these names, or like-sounding ones, into a narrative where they have not previously appeared. Thus the chief character of Finnish rune songs, Väinämöinen, has entered Estonian mythology in the distorted form Vanemuine. In the same way, Odin's name has appeared in Swedish narrations, even in Finland.

In certain cases even genuine folk materials must be set aside for special treatment. For example, if an international tale has been altered into a ballad by one people, then the variants of this ballad may not be placed on the same level as the prose variants of this

---

[2] *Finnisch-ugrische Forschungen*, VII (1908), 181.
[3] Kaarle Krohn, *Skandinavisk mytologi* (Helsinki, 1922), p. 20.

tale. They must first be compared with each other in order to determine the basic form of the ballad. This basic form then represents the tale form from which the ballad emanated and only this one may be compared directly with other Märchen prose variants.

Finally, those transcriptions must be treated separately where doubts arise as to whether they can truly be counted as variants of the traditional forms under investigation. In order to be able to differentiate genetic correspondences from incidental similarities, we require a certain knowledge of the kinds and degrees of identity, to which a later chapter is directed.

Above all, the *oral*, *genuine*, and *actual* variations of the selected themes are to be assembled. Even the literary, less reliable, and only partially corresponding materials must be worked with and given due attention, even though they have been separated from the central mass.

VI. Arranging the Materials

AFTER THE ASSEMBLED MATERIALS have been surveyed, they must still be arranged for utilization. Literary documents are usually arranged chronologically. They are labeled with an abbreviated name for the manuscript, for the printed copy, or for the author.

Folk variants are generally arranged according to language—their most distinguishing characteristic. Since the language of the transcription is as a rule stated, even in translation, one never need be uncertain about this factor. Within one and the same linguistic area, a further division can be made according to towns and villages if these are given or if they can be ascertained. Any connection between traditional ethnographic and more modern geographic boundaries is, strictly speaking, inconsequential. It is, however, useful and to some degree scientifically justified. Ethnographic areas were once geographically connected.

Wherever immigration has occurred, language as well as traditions have also migrated. Thus Finnish settlers on the border between Sweden and Norway around 1600 preserved the beliefs and folklore of their Savo homeland, which were much richer than the materials that they later borrowed from their Swedish and Norwegian neighbors.

Linguistic classification furthermore offers the advantage of the briefest and most readily learned annotation. European languages and nations can be sorted with few exceptions into six groups labeled with their initial letters:

C = Celtic	R = Romance
F = Finno-Ugric	S = Slavic
G = Germanic	T = Turko-Tataric

The second letter suffices in most other cases to designate special language groups and nations, including closely related ones:

CB = Breton	CS = Scots Gaelic
CI = Irish	CW = Welsch
FE = Estonian	FU = Ugrian—near the Urals
FF = Finnish	(Voguls, Ostyaks)
FL = Lapp	FW = Volga tribes (Mord-
FM = Magyar	vinians, Cheremissians)
FP = Permian (Zyrians, Votyaks)	
GD = Danish	GN = Norwegian
GE = English	GS = Swedish
GG = German	GSF (or simply GF) = Swedish-
GH = Dutch	speaking Germanic Finns
GI = Icelandic	GV = Flemish
RE = Spanish	RL = Rhaeto-Romanic (Ladin,
RF = French	Friulian)

RI = Italian	RP = Portuguese
	RR = Rumanian
SB = Bulgarian	SS = Serbian, Croatian, and
SČ = Czech and Slovak	Slovenian
SP = Polish	SU = Ukrainian and Ruthenian
SR = Russian	SW = Wendish
SRW = White Russian	

A few European peoples will have to be symbolized with the first three letters of their language name:

Alb = Albanian	Let = Lettish
Bas = Basque	Lit = Lithuanian
Gre = Greek	Sam = Samoyed

With three—at the most, four—letters one can temporarily get by with such abbreviations even for non-European names because of the very restricted numbers, especially if an abbreviation for a major world division precedes it: As, Af, Am, or Au. Besides countries in which both the names of the language and the countries are the same (such as Arm = Armenian, Arab = Arabic), countries that represent political areas with diverse languages and ethnic areas are used (such as Ind = India). In a future systematization of non-European symbols, one must consider whether better-known geographic names are to be preferred to the diverse ethnographic ones.

The use of two capital letters for the most frequently represented European linguistic areas carries with it the advantage that a more precise geographic designation can be attained, typographically, with lower-case letters. Finnish variants especially demand such an addition, not only because of their great number, but also because of the typical difference between West Finnish and East Finnish traditions. This additional lower-case letter designates the Finnish linguistic areas of Sweden and Russia as well as the various political and geographic regions of Finland itself.

If several variants are transcribed in one linguistic area or, more precisely, in the selfsame geographic locale, they must be assigned a classification number. This may suggest a complete numbering of all collected variants. Since, however, new variants frequently appear during a project, they would cause a continual displacement of the previously assigned numbers.[1] Also, in a continuous number series, three-digit numbers would be highly troublesome as soon as one attempted to arrange a sequential index of variants with diverse characteristics.

Since linguistic areas do not always correspond with geographic ones, Reidar Th. Christiansen has tried (FFC No. 24) to introduce boldface characters for various parts of Europe; like the continental designations, they should be placed before the ethnographic abbreviations. So far he has applied these in only a few extensive indexes. Even without these characters the variants could be enumerated in geographic order by separately indicating the logogram of the same linguistic area or even of the same language. Thus Magyar (FM), Siebenbürger-Saxon (GG), Rumanian (RR), and Bulgarian (SB) variants that geographically belong to the Balkan and Eastern European area are separated from the other Finno-Ugric, Germanic (and for that matter German), Romance, and Slavic variants and are numbered in sequence.

Most important is to carry out consistently a definite classification of each and every occurrence of a variant. The index of variants, from which all abbreviated designations obtain their rationale, must be arranged either in this same manner or according to an alphabetical ordering of the symbols. Thus, without difficulty an interested reader may also seek more precise indications of the place, time, or type of a transcription and, if its content is also abstracted, he can inform himself about the relationship of analytically treated traits with a minimum of effort.

In investigating folklore material that is primarily restricted to

---

[1] If necessary, if no further re-ordering of numbers is possible, a few additions could be made by means of appending, for example, a Greek letter in the appropriate places.

one linguistic area, the principle of classifying variants according to geography has its greatest relevance. The magical rune songs of the Finns, which can still be recorded today in all Finnish linguistic areas, have been arranged in accordance with the geographic divisions applied to Finnish Märchen. A simple lower-case letter with a classification number has been used as a symbol for rune variants. In certain cases, however, a more precise statement of the parish has been necessary. Old districts in the Middle Ages probably represented both ethnographic and geographic units. At the onset of the modern age, however, a colonization of the Savo (f,g) segregated from the region of West Finnish dialects and traditions, not only northern Tavastland, which as a whole can be joined with all of East Finland under one designation (e), but also a few neighboring parishes in Northern Satakunta (b) and Southern Oesterbotne (k).

A special division is required for the scientific treatment of the epic rune songs preserved chiefly by Karelian singers: in Archangel (p) and Olonetz (q); in North (j), East (i), and South (h) Finnish Karelia; as well as in North (s), Mid (t), and West (u) Ingermanland. The song styles of each parish and, in Archangel, even those of every individual village are differentiated by obvious characteristics, especially in the first four "northern" song areas (p, q, j, i), where ancient heroic lays have been most perfectly preserved. Since these tiny but very important districts must be continually noted in any research, practical, abbreviated symbols for their names are necessary.

The more bounded an area is, the greater the possibility that a traditional item recorded within its boundaries is not indigenous to it but rather has been imported from another region—usually a neighboring one—that was the former home or temporary residence of the transmitter or his informant. In such cases this district designation should be added in brackets with the symbol <.

Estonian rune songs, a complete edition of which was recently begun, are arranged and labeled in such a way that they can be cited in scholarly works without additional abbreviation. That each song keep its main number is not especially important, since usually a song is studied in and of itself. Variants are arranged according to regions and, within these, according to parishes. The symbol for an individual transcription consists of two initials for the name of the region as well as the classification number, which is continuous only for variants in a relevant area, not for all variants of the song; therefore, this number seldom exceeds two digits.

In publishing Finnish animal tales I tried to group variants first according to typology, either according to the main characters (for instance, the bear, the wolf, or the fox) or according to some other basic characteristic, such as housing—for example, domestic animals building a house in the forest (Bremen City Musicians). In both of these cases, I chose the most obvious characteristics of the differences between southwestern and northeastern Finnish variants stemming from Scandinavian and Russian influences.

The advantage of such emphasis of a single, albeit important trait above all others, however, is slight when compared to the inconvenience of documenting a cited variant and comparing quoted transcriptions from one and the same area.

A sample of this procedure is offered in Lutz Mackensen's Märchen study *The Singing Bones* (FFC no. 49). After one to three initial letters of the language, such as *F* for French or *Sp* for Spanish, he gives the classification number. But this is not a continuing series for the linguistic area; instead it is divided according to succeeding typological signs. *F1b* to *F4b* are French variants of the tree (Baum) form; in another place we find references *F1k* through *F15k* for bone (Knochen) types. A further attempt at a typological arrangement consists of arranging the numbering within the sequence according to the relationship between the variant in question and the assumed archetype. With this procedure, the study of the basic form must be conducted before numbers are assigned to the variants. Without some numbering, however, the study cannot even be begun; assignment of temporary numbers, on the other hand, causes the unnecessary trouble of continual re-arrangement. More serious considerations are caused by the fact that the assumed basic form may be more closely reflected by one variant in one respect, by another variant in another respect, and that the relative completeness and authenticity of the reference materials, as well as the more or less subjective judgment of the folklorist, play a part in the determination of the original form.

Whatever else may also be true, the purely external *ethnographic and geographic classification* of variants collected in the field has the advantage of practical applicability and objectivity.

VII. Establishing Geographic Classifications

IT HAS BEEN RECOGNIZED for a long time that the linguistic frame of a tradition is directly connected with the modification of its contents. We can observe in transcriptions collected from colonial enclaves in which foreign languages are spoken that folklore migrates through time and space along with language. The diffusion of words from generation to generation within one language cannot be compared with the transmission of the content of the traditions in either their extent or age. Rather, the transmission of these folk traditions can best be compared with transmission of culture words that are carried from one language to another and that also migrate within a language, by borrowing, from dialect to dialect.

The search for common legends with common elements among the Finno-Ugric peoples has not produced any results. Nor have Finno-Mordvinian analogues been found. To date, research in the Indo-European sphere has remained equally unproductive.

In classifying the fox tale I arranged Finnish transcriptions, as I have already mentioned, according to the main character, fox, bear, or wolf, from the Southwest to the Northeast, according to Scandinavian and Russian forms. Later it was repeatedly reaffirmed that West Finnish tales generally belong with the Swedish variants and East Finnish ones with the Russian variants. As stated, we can find in one and the same geographic area in Southeastern Europe representatives of most large European language groups that possess in common not only a similar inventory of fairy tales but also to a great extent similar forms of one and the same fairy tale.

The significance of and justification for geographic classification was first grasped by Julius Krohn in his *Kalevala* work. He found that every region possesses its own song style and that, in addition, differences or similarities in song styles between various regions are in direct relationship to the relative distance between these regions. This fact can be explained only by accepting the principle of geographic diffusion in which the variations, shown in regional song styles, increase progressively in the direction of migration.

Even Benfey gave great weight to the migration of folk narratives, but he thought that this migration was accomplished primarily through literature. Of course there are some widely broadcast Märchen, such as *Ingratitude Is the World's Reward*, whose folk variants with few exceptions have sprung from literary origins. With these tales, however, geographic classification of variants, which is characteristic of all tales of genuine oral transmission, is absent.[1]

Oral diffusion of folklore outside its area of origin can of course be achieved through the migration of a whole community or of sin-

[1] Kaarle Krohn, *Mann und Fuchs* (*Commentationes Variae . . . Universitas Helsingforsiensis*, no. 4) (Helsinki, 1891), pp. 42–47.

gle persons, especially as the result of marriage. Temporary visits by hunters, fishermen, craftsmen, merchants, sailors, soldiers, pilgrims, or other wanderers also must be considered. Of greater importance, however, is the steady influence of the constant movement within a neighborhood. Up until the modern age, the country peoples of Europe were bound to the soil. The diffusion of their traditions took place orally "through the folk mouth," from farm to farm, village to village, parish to parish, in a continuous chain of neighborly contacts. Like coins passing from hand to hand, traditions migrated from mouth to mouth.

It is not hard to trace geographic variation chains in international Märchen. The longer the road traveled, the more numerous were the factors causing transformations.

Of course, occasional similarities are encountered between variants of widely separated peoples that have never been in contact with each other. If it is not a question of a shared prototype, long lost, then consideration must be given to the possibility of independent variations or creations at the new site—evidence perhaps of the parallel workings of human fantasy. Such correspondences are above all like those of phonetically similar, onomatopoetic words that are occasionally encountered when totally different languages are compared.

Conversely, variants of a single tale that differ considerably from each other as a result of decaying recollection, an active, continuing folk imagination, and, above all, a diverse blending with other tale materials can be found among closely related peoples or in adjacent areas.

In order to be able to judge correctly the correspondences in treating a traditional theme from two geographic areas, we must determine the pattern structure to which the individual variants of each area may be traced. In order to pursue the full development of an item yet further, we must seek the *archetype* of the collective variants.

VIII. Procedure of Analysis

THE DETERMINATION of the basic form of a tradition, along with its local pattern form, requires an *analytical* study of its variants, feature by feature, in geographic order. On the technical side, this analysis must not require excessive time and it must be lucid.

Each variation of a verse line in a rhymed folk poem or variation of a feature, as well as each detail of unrhymed materials, is noted down with the identifying mark of the variants in which it occurs. Loose sheets of paper used on one side only are the most convenient format. If the number of variations together with their examples require more than one page of whatever format is chosen, a new page should be used. In any case one must have constant access to a quick survey, which does not exist when both sides of the sheet are used.

Variations are recorded in each listing in the same order, in keeping with a strict serial sequence of variants. Certain simplified phrases can be used for the wording of variations, as well as symbols for the citations; they can save one a good deal of work and at the same time provide ready access.

In the Märchen of King Thrushbeard (FFC No. 50, pp. 12–13), the main character varies in the French (RF1–3), the German (GG1–16), and the Danish versions (GD1–7) in the following manner:

Prince of France	RF1, RF2, GG15
King of France	RF3
King without named country	GG1, GG2, GG3, GG13
King of Prussia	GG4
Prince without named country	GG5, GG6, GG7, GG8, GG9, GG10, GG14, GG16, GD1, GD6
Prince of England	GG11
Fritz of Prussia	GG12
Young Lord without named country	GD2
Prince of Denmark	GD3, GD4
King of Denmark	GD5, GD7

These variations can be indexed from the very start in a way that is easier for the hand as well as for the eye:

Prince of France	RF1, 2; GG15
King of France	RF3
King ——	GG1, 2, 3; GG13
King of Prussia	GG4
Prince ——	GG5, 6, 7, 8, 9, 10, 14, 16; GD1, 6
Prince of England	GG11

Fritz of Prussia	GG12
Young Lord ———	GD2
Prince of Denmark	GD3, 4
King of Denmark	GD5, 7

In order to set forth the relationships of variations to each other in a way more easily scanned, they should be transcribed in an order dictated by their contents:

Prince of France	RF1, 2; GG15
King of France	RF3
Prince of England	GG11
Prince of Denmark	GD3, 4
King of Denmark	GD5, 7
King of Prussia	GG4
Fritz of Prussia	GG12
Prince ———	GG5–10, 14, 16; GD1, 6
King ———	GD1–3; GG13
Young Lord ———	GD2

When indexing verse variations, it is not necessary from a folkloristic point of view to note all purely formal, phonetic, or orthographic deviations. By grouping verse forms that differ only in insignificant details, one avoids more than an unnecessary waste of time; facility in scanning the array is also improved when words with their meanings stand out, unobscured by dialect aberrations.

In Finnish rune songs, which express virtually every thought in two or more verses with all manner of words, the classification may also vary. If the parallel verses are identified with numbers or letters, the variations within the series can also be easily marked in the same way.

The arrangement of the various components of a story can be studied in the same way. W. Anderson labeled the numerous combinations of riddles in the jest about the Emperor and the Abbot (FFC No. 42, pp. 266–277) by using capital letters as well as numbers (for the various formulations) and arranged them in lexicon style so that any synthesis along with its references can be spotted immediately.

The purpose of this analytic procedure, as stated, is the determination of the ur-form of any characteristic of the theme under study as well as the original combination and arrangement of these traits in order to determine the basic form as well as the pattern form in various areas; from the relationship between the basic form and the pattern form, the route of diffusion and development of the tradition in question can be discovered.

In order to be able to draw the correct conclusions from analytically prepared materials, we still need an awareness of the laws that are generative in the development of products of the folk imagination as well as of those laws that are instrumental in temporal diffusion and spatial distribution, all of which are manifest in the kaleidoscopic variations of folklore.

IX. The Influence of Faulty Memory

IF WE OBSERVE the laws whose effects are recognizable in the manifold modifications of the original form of a tradition, we encounter first the influence of faulty memory. This can be seen most clearly in repeated transcriptions of a rather long epic lay that features continuous lines without strophic division.

Forgetting can, first of all, be momentary. It is indeed difficult to keep a series of verse lines in mind in the same order at any particular time, especially during the unexpected visit of a field worker. A verse or a group of verses does not always appear in its correct place in the memory, but rather somewhat later in the song, which brings about a displacement of song segments. During an occasional recitation a verse belonging to a particular song can be omitted. Even during an immediate repetition of a performance this verse may appear, or a verse recited during the first recall may be forgotten in the second. More mutations take place in various recitations by the same singer if the recitations are separated by a relatively long period of time.

The influence of forgetfulness is even more apparent when transcriptions from an older singer and his heirs, especially during an era marked by a decline in song tradition, are compared. Of the great Sampo Song the most prominent singers in Archangel Karelia remembered: Arhippa Perttunen in Latvajärvi (1834), 401 verses and Ontrei Malinen in Vuonninen (1833), 366 verses. Forty years later (1871 and 1877) the son of the former, Miihkali, recalled 293 and 338 verses respectively, and the youngest son of the latter, Jyrki, 313 and 363. At the same time (1872) Ontrei's grandchildren produced 129 (Iivana) and 175 (Jeremei) verses.

The number of mistakes of memory increases significantly when the song is not inherited directly but is transmitted instead to a neighbor who has joined the singing during a visit or during a common task or has been taught the songs during revels; finally it may be passed along to an outsider who only occasionally hears it. Thus the song is transmitted to yet others, and forgetting plays an ever-greater role.

In the Finnish rune songs, where every verse is accompanied by one or more parallel verses, one of these can be omitted without damaging the contents noticeably. From Arhippa Perttunen's description of the striking of the Lapp arrow

> Through the flesh of the collarbone
> From the right shoulder
> Through the left armpit,

his son Miihkali had dropped the middle line by 1871 and the last one by 1877. In a couplet, a part of the two parallel verses can also disappear. The gaps can then be stopped with meaningless fillers:

I cannot forge the Sampo,
Decorate the beautiful covers.

becomes

I cannot, I myself, forge
Nor decorate the covers.

Occasionally a verse-pair can shrink to one:

To the scrub-pine from the elm,
Near the Smithy Ilmarinen

becomes

To the scrub-pine of Ilmarinen

Finally, a verse pair can simply vanish from the memory.

Details superfluous to the main theme are the first to disappear from the contents of an epic song as well as from a prose narrative. Introductions and conclusions seem to be especially vulnerable to this danger. Thus, in several variations of the Märchen about the man who can talk with animals (FFC No. 15) the description of his learning the language of the animals is missing; it is assumed without elaboration that the man possesses this wonderful skill. In some transcriptions of the Märchen of the Singing Bones (FFC No. 49), the logical punishment of the murderess at the story's conclusion is similarly omitted.

Even an essential trait can fall by the wayside if the plot can persist without it. In the farce about the Emperor and the Abbot (FFC No. 42), the contrast between the Prelate and the Novice who gives the required answers vanishes when the answerer blends with the questioner into one personality.

In addition, the substitution of the chief verse with parallel lines in Finnish rune verse pairs can be traced to forgetfulness. In two rhymed verse pairs there can also be a reversal of main verses and parallel verses. In the Finnish songs about the creation of the world, the sun (V.2) is said to spring from the egg white (V.1) and the moon (V.4) from the yolk (V.3). But conversely the egg white is also connected with the moon and the yolk with the sun (V.1 + 4 + 3 + 2 or 3 + 2 + 1 + 4). In the same way individual traits in the prose narrative can exchange places. In the Märchen about the Magic Ring,[1] sometimes the dog perversely sits on the back of the cat. In variants of the Bremen City Musicians Märchen (FFC No. 11) the locations of the animals in night quarters as well as the human occupations that they seem to represent in the imagination of the intruders are interchanged in many combinations.

Generalizations of individual traits must also be described as partial loss of recall. In the farce about the Man from Paradise (FFC No. 22), the Parisian student sometimes fades into a common traveler. The kind of tree is easily forgotten, and a precise number frequently deteriorates into an indeterminate plural. The well-known riddle about man—"In the morning it goes on four feet, during the day on three feet [sic], at evening on two feet [sic]"—is simplified to "first," "then," and "finally" (FFC No. 27, p. 15).

Simplification should also be included here. In the Finnish song about the singing contest, young Joukahainen originally offers old Väinämöinen two boats, two horses, and his only sister. Later this difference in numbers was forgotten, and the number in each wager was generalized to two or simply to one.

Forgetting a detail that is essential to the contents weakens logical cohesion and soon causes new holes in the narration. After the questioner and answerer in the farce about the Emperor and the Abbot faded into one person, the required deadline was also dropped as unnecessary (FFC No. 42, p. 251).

Where there is a poor memory, the thread of the narrative itself may be broken—either in the middle so that the conclusion is lost or even in the beginning so that the story starts in the middle. Both situations can occur in the same tale, with the result that only the central section is left. In this way *fragments* come into being. The

---

[1] A. Aarne, *Vergleichende Märchenforschung* (*Mémoires de la Société Finno-ougrienne*, no. 25) (Helsinki, 1908).

Finnish song about Sampo is recited in complete form only in Archangel Karelia. In northern Finnish Karelia the introduction and conclusion are sung as separate songs; the middle section has not been preserved. In eastern Finnish Karelia we find the introduction, but only a few verses of the conclusion and then in a completely different context. Among Savo immigrants in Sweden, only a short summary of the conclusion is noted in a few verse pairs. In the remaining Finnish song areas not a single fragment of this song is encountered.

In the event that no trace of a folk tradition can be detected in a certain area and yet it seems possible that it existed there at one time, it is important to be able to determine the circumstances under which such a hypothesis can be advanced. The assumption is probable if the area in question lies between two others that are not in direct contact but that do preserve the same tradition. The smaller the interposed area, the more certain the assumption that the tradition in question previously migrated through the region and that it was once diffused throughout it. A colony that is surrounded by foreign language areas can bear witness to the previous existence of a tradition in a country where it has since been forgotten. The fragment of the Sampo song that was collected from Savo colonists in Sweden proves that this song was also sung in the Finnish area of Savo around 1600.

A further argument for former knowledge of a tradition within the region in question is the variants from another region which contain idioms and words, natural phenomena and ethnographic relationships that are relevant to the former but not to the latter region. One hundred years ago Lönnrot's predecessor, Z. Topelius, Sr., called attention to the fact that the presence of the oak in the songs of Archangel Karelia indicates a more southerly home of the songs. In the Sampo song mentioned above we find, not only a few anomalous idioms and words, but also the custom of plowing with oxen, a practice unknown to Karelins or to East Finns in general;

this is evidence of the migration of the song from Southwest Finland, where the old heroic song has long been absent.

If we have some idea of the general direction of the diffusion of songs or tales within a country or between two countries, then the assumption that a song was forgotten in individual cases at the source of the migration is more justifiable. The rune song in Archangel Karelia is restricted to the one district that adjoins the Finnish border; according to the unanimous evidence of all the circumstances the songs entered there from the Finnish side. All details that have been investigated up to the present of East Finnish variants point in this same direction, to the west. On the other hand, we have no reason to assume that rune songs were sung earlier in Karelian regions where they are not now present.

The song about the virgin who is to be ransomed migrated from Sweden to Finland as well as to Estonia in varying, independent forms. A closely related and apparently contemporary song about a bartered virgin occurs in both Finnish and Estonian versions; the similarities, as well as the differences, can be explained only by postulating a common source. This source, the basic form of both versions, must have been Swedish, even though it has not yet been proved to exist in Scandinavia.

A chain narrative about the hen and the rooster, which immigrated from Sweden to Finland, has been collected almost exclusively in the region of the West Finnish dialect. Of course, a few variants have also been encountered in the East Finnish dialect. However, if these are to be explained as exceptions, be it because they occur close to the dialect border or to the western home of the informant or because the song has been learned from a chapbook, then we have a complete lack of genuine East Finnish examples. The direction of diffusion, in this particular case as well as in general, excludes the assumption that this lack was caused by the atrophy of the narrative within the folk repertory.

The later traditions remain vital, and the more complete their collection, the less cause we have to assume something existed that has since been forgotten. In Estonia the old rune songs are still fostered in our day and have been preserved for us by all parishes in approximately seventy thousand variants. If from this mass of transcriptions no parallels for a particular Finnish song can be found, then some extraordinarily weighty arguments must be put forward if we attempt to explain the absence in terms of its having been forgotten.

On the basis of O. Kallas' inquiry, T. Okkola[2] wrote an article on the extinction of the rune song in modern Estonia. The modern form of the folksong has not supplanted the old rune song here as the single-strophe lyric has in Finland. Folksongs with end-rhyme (new examples of which have penetrated old-style rhyme and meter) that have arisen since the eighteenth century have not encroached upon the predominant position of the rune song. Actually only the art-song taught in folk-schools has infringed on its territory. Not even religious songs previously introduced by the Church have disturbed the rune song, with the exception of a few parishes where pietism has attained general favor. The folksong is rarely disturbed by governmental authority; there are, however, a few cases of legal punishment imposed because of the specially derisive contents of some folksongs. Even a taskmaster could take delight in song and grant a singer leave from work. Work itself was advanced by choral song. As a whole the era of serfdom, with its closely adjacent dwellings, common workshops, and common fields, was advantageous for the conservation of traditional song. With the freeing of the peasants came the dispersion of their homes and fields. Festive gatherings—especially weddings—kept certain genres of songs in use for a while. But large weddings, with their many customs, also began to disappear. Finally there was the World War and the [Russian—trans.] Revolution, which directed the interest of the people toward outside affairs and left little room for old memories.

2 *Suomi*, V(2), 211–247.

X. The Impulse toward Expansion

THE ANTITHESIS OF FORGETTING, the tendency toward expansion, either is caused by the very act of forgetting or emanates from an urge to spontaneity. Additions to a tradition can be either new inventions or borrowings from some other context.

Enlargement is also illustrated in the recitations of Finnish rune singers at different times and through succeeding generations. Arhippa Perttunen, mentioned above, has old Väinämöinen, who winds up in the sea as a result of the Lapp's shot, driven by the wind into *dark Polijola* "Nordheim." His son sang the same verse in 1871 and added from the Lemminkäinen cycle: "to the isle on the open sea, to the treeless land." But in 1877 he had dropped not only this addition but also the original verse and had replaced them with a verse pair from the song about the Great Oak: "to the nameless bay, whose name is known to no one."

The simplest kind of expansion in the rune song consists of repetition of a verse or verse group. The verse "up to old Väinämöinen," which regularly concludes the description of the anger of the squint-eyed Lapp, has occasionally been added to the description of the construction of the bow. A question posed on encounter can be repeated by means of the introduction of new persons who are to give the reply. In the Estonian song about the banished geese, a plowman in the fields is as a rule the person asked; later, hay workers, herdsmen, and others were added as additional targets for interrogation.[1]

Under the heading of repetition must also be reckoned the exposition in the third person of a challenge delivered in the second person, a report in the third person and an answer in the first person to a question in the second person. These types of repetition could have been original in some songs or late additions in others, as O. Kallas has demonstrated in his study of repetitive songs in Estonian folk poetry.

Duplication or multiplication of some element is a common occurrence. In the tale *The Bear Catches the Fish*, in addition to the vent hole in the ice in which the bear breaks off his tail, there appears now and then another episode in which the sly fox sits with his tail carefully held aloft. In the earlier adventure of the fox feigning death, sometimes only one fisherman makes an appearance, but at other times the number of passersby is multiplied and only the last lifts the fox onto his cart.[2] In the Estonian song about the dismembered oxen, the bear appears in parallel verses, instead of his epithet "broadpaws," in addition to the original

[1] Oskar Kallas, *Die Widerholungslieder*, I (*Mémoires de la Société Finno-ougrienne* XVI, no. 1) (1901), p. 217.
[2] *Journal de la Société Finno-ougrienne*, VI (1889), 33, 44, 49.

wolf, although in reality they do not share company. Sometimes great crowds of both species have been formed from this one bear and one wolf.[3]

It is quite unnecessary for the hen, or several of them, to accompany the rooster without any special task in the tale *The Animals on the Road* (FFC No. 11). In other variants of this tale, when wild animals join domestic ones in their forest quarters, the fundamental nature of the Märchen is contradicted.

Additions can also consist of many kinds of elaborations and rationalizations. In several Estonian variants of the song that immigrated from Finland, about Prudish Marketta and her seducer, her innocence is sworn not only by general oaths but, indeed, by oaths that damn body and soul to hell—more precisely, to the boiling cauldrons of hell.[4] In the legend about the man throwing his knife into a whirlwind during hay harvest a note is sometimes added, to explain how he happened to have a knife in his hand, that he was resting during mowing and was either using the knife to eat with or was cutting a drinking cup out of birch bark.

Enlargement corresponds to the truncation of a narrative thread. In the chain tale about the choking rooster, the hen usually runs directly to fetch water. This introduction is expanded in many Danish variants for the reason that the tomcat appears in place of the rooster. Of course milk must be brought to the cat and this is promised by the cow, if, in turn, water is brought to her. In the usual Finnish version, the rooster faints in a hot bathhouse and needs the water to be revived. In some variants the rooster does not have steam for bathing. This is requested by the hen from the bathhouse stove, which in turn needs water for its hot stones. In the middle of this same chain tale, meal is to be brought to the brewer by the miller, who, for his part, needs grain from the fields. This middleman episode is sometimes enlarged in Finland in such a way that the brewer demands malt from the malter, the malter meal

---

[3] *Mémoires de la Société Finno-ougrienne*, no. 16, p. 129.
[4] *Finnish-ugrische Forschungen*, XVI, 122.

from the miller, the miller grain from the thresher, and the thresher the harvest from the fields. The chain ends with the charcoal burner who provides charcoal for the smith, without any further demands for himself. In one Danish variant, however, the chain is extended by the wish of the charcoal burner for fire, which is to be obtained from hell.

The desire to expand is also manifested in the riddle about the year (FFC No. 26, pp. 136, 141). The common European form goes:

> There is a tree,
> Which has twelve twigs (months)
> And on each twig four nests (weeks)
> And in each nest seven eggs (days).

In an Estonian version it continues:

> From each egg twenty-four chicks (hours);
> Each chick has sixty feathers (minutes),
> Each feather sixty fluffs (seconds).

In contrast to generalization caused by forgetting is *specialization*, which gives to some element a new nuance. An unnamed person without home or occupation receives a name, citizenship, and position. A tree of no particular kind becomes a specific type.

In the Grimm Märchen *The Ragamuffin* and *Lord Korbes* (Nos. 10 and 41), variants of an older form of the theme "The Animals on the Road," we find a knitting needle and a pin that, through simultaneous doubling and specialization, stemmed from one needle. In a Flemish transcription there are even three particular kinds of needles—the third being a darning needle (FFC No. 11, p. 95). In the Finnish rune song about the poor servant girl and the rich landlord (the Lazarus theme), both of their souls are usually brought by the same angels to the same heaven, where they are then assigned different fates. In later variants, both the collecting angels and the destination have split into two, with the soul of the landlord being carried to hell by devils. The forms of death are basically different: the servant girl dies outside in the snow and cold, the landlord at home in bed. Through the forgetting of the last manner of death, many variations have the landlord die on the "hard snow crust" or "in the terrible weather." But in some variants the urge for differentiation again occurs. Either, in contrast to the inapplicable motivation of the servant's thin clothing, drunkenness is given as the reason for the landlord's freezing, or he dies outside "on his hard gold coins."[5]

In order to expand the depiction, as mentioned, additions are usually borrowed from other forms of traditional lore that have been preserved in folk memory. Segments of various folklore items that contain identical or similar characteristics are easily bound together. The uniting knot can occur in almost any word or phrase. A familiar noun in a variant of Finnish creation runes compares the description of the hatching of a duck egg "like a duck her ducklings," which because of the complete correspondence of the compared items is out of place. It has been borrowed from a historical song about Pontus de la Gardie, whose array of ships on the sea is compared with that of ducklings. In the Finnish rune song about sowing barley, the tiller of the soil is described by the adjectives "small, short, slim." A couplet of a lyric song in which the smallness of a child is illustrated through comparison with the mother's distaff and the father's knee has been attached to this. After the golden world egg has been increased to six golden eggs, this number has acquired in some Archangel variants an addition, a seventh egg of iron. This accretion was borrowed from a Finnish riddle about the six workdays of the week and Sunday: "six eggs, the seventh an iron egg" (FFC No. 26, p. 131). The remembrance of a former time has connected the introductory verse of the song about the freeing of heaven's light, "formerly people lived without the sun," with the lines of a lyric song with a similar beginning, "formerly people lived behind a stream, ate

---

[5] *Journal de la Société Finno-ougrienne*, LII, 129.

fish," etc. The above examples have both adverb and verb in common. Most frequently, compounding is induced by a similar plot. In the Finnish Sampo Song we find several such combinations. The mention of the lament of Väinämöinen, who has been driven into the sea, has attracted many different mournful songs. To describe the Sampo watchers' falling asleep, similar passages have been borrowed from various other songs: the influence of the warming sun is from the legend of the resurrection of the Savior; the harp playing is from the song of Katharina who defends her honor against the troubador Vetrikka; and the sleep-inducing magic needle is from the Märchen. To the smearing of the lock with fat and opening it with the fingers has been associated the smearing of the door hinge with beer from the song about Katharina and Vetrikka mentioned above, the coiling through the crevices from Väinämöinen's return from the underworld, and the breaking of the lock from the Finnish version of the bylina about Ivan Godinovitsch.

In the event that a large section of one traditional item is affixed to the end of another, a continuation results that extends beyond the framework of the latter. Its connection can be brought about in a purely mechanical fashion. This is the case in the recitation of a single-strophe lyric in which one strope can follow another, unchanged in any order, however the strophe comes to mind. The desire for free arrangement of some lyric themata is also manifested in the Finnish-Estonian rune song. Magic runes in East Finland have developed, not only by means of detailed description, but also by the linking together of various parallel narratives about the origins of the same evil subject. In Ingermanland, epic rune songs have blended together in such manifold ways that the plan to arrange them according to their contents had to be abandoned in order to avoid twofold or threefold repetition in most of the transcriptions. In Finnish Karelia and Archangel the unions are of a more fixed kind. Especially in the latter area the song complexes center about certain heroes' names.

In the successive singing of two rather long songs, violence to both can seldom be avoided. Usually the first is truncated and the second takes up at the point where they share a common characteristic. The second song can also be interrupted in turn, if a third song or the conclusion of the first song is joined at some point of contact. In the latter case the second song is enclosed by the first as if in a frame. Among Archangel singers the Sampo Song, which has incorporated various other songs, constitutes a frame of this sort. This framing was further developed by Lönnrot in the *Kalevala.*

Two Finnish runes about the origins of the world have been composed about the creation of fire; they occur linked together as well as incorporated within each other. In one, fire descends into a room after it strikes from heaven. The fire hurts a mother and child there. In the other, fire has fallen from its crib in heaven and has caused mischief in the water. These basic characteristics have been combined in various versions in almost every conceivable way (FFC No. 52, p. 119):

A. striking of fire—harm in the room—cradle—mischief in water
B. striking of fire—in water—cradle—harm in room
C. striking of fire—cradle—harm in room—in water
D. cradle—striking of fire—harm in room—in water

The number of possible combinations has been increased still further by omission of one of the four elements, usually the striking of the fire or the cradle—events that are harder to conceive of, directly following each other, than the two acts of destruction.

In the Märchen we also find successive ordering of adventures of the same kind, as well as firm unions of various themata, with one of them usually forfeiting something of its content in the union.

XI. Laws of Transformation

FORGETTING OR OBSCURING a trait often creates, per se, a transformation—as does the addition of a new trait or the clarification of one already present. If the forgetting and addition work together, the transformation becomes even more obvious. When the answer to a riddle is forgotten, a new, appropriate answer must be invented. A singer who cannot remember a word of a song must substitute a synonym, if the sense of the term is retained in his mind, or some other word that fits the context. When a parallel verse is dropped from a Finnish rune song, usually there is a substitution of a new parallel verse.

Forgetting and adding are of course not the only factors giving rise to variation. Whoever has learned to sing a song has perhaps missed or mistaken some word. Or a word that he has heard correctly is from some earlier stage of the language or foreign dialect so that it is hard for him to pick it up with its correct pronunciation. Then it is either mutilated into some incomprehensible phonetic combination or it becomes dependent on some other, more familiar word. An ancient designation for the sacrificial ale, *kahja*, has been altered through folk etymology by Archangel rune singers, who know nothing of traditional brewing, to *kalja*, "weak beer," or *kahvi*, "coffee."

Names are especially subject to all kinds of distortion. The saint's name Hubertus, which is alien to the Finnish tongue, has been variously revised in magic runes not only phonetically, which is encouraged further by alliteration in rune verses—for example, Huupero, Hyperä, Huikurja, Huitua, Kuitua, Kuihtana—but also transformed in accordance with words of known meaning—for example, Kuippana ("long neck"), Kulkija ("wanderer"), Kummutar ("daughter of the forest hill"). A medieval West Finnish song that immigrated to Ingermanland and that tells about the dragon with the virgin contains the expression "war with Denmark." Since this geographic concept scarcely exists among singers there today, in most variants the name, *Tanimarkki*, has been changed in some way; for example, to Tani-Martti ("Daniel Martin").

Occasionally a foreign dialect expression that is still comprehensible has been translated into another word more common in the native dialect. In the Ingermanland song mentioned above, the West Finnish word *yrkä* (genitive *yrjän*) occasionally is replaced by the word *sulho*, both meaning "bridegroom"; *yrkä* in turn has replaced the name Yrjänä ("George") in the West Finnish prototype through folk etymology.

On the other hand, without the slightest change of the phonetic form, a new dialect interpretation can give a completely new direction to the sense of the material. In a lyric song that migrated to Ingermanland from Estonia, proper sequence in singing is equated with the duty of the community to keep mounts ready for travelers. The Estonian word for "district" in the Finnish form *valta* is still current in West Ingermanland; in Central and Eastern Finland it is understood in the sense of "government." The original utterance of the singer, which she was obligated to sing in proper sequence just as the village is to assist the traveler and the district to exchange horses, has been semantically altered so that the government is obligated in sequence to provide traveling money.

Furthermore, transformation causes an inclination in the transmission of a piece of foreign folklore to assume a local context. The pun on Paris/paradise in the farce about the scholar who profits from the misunderstanding of a simple landlady (FFC No. 22) has been changed in a Southwest Finnish variant in such a way that the phonetically similar, more familiar parish Parainen (Elative "out of": Paraisista < Pariisista) replaces Paris. Even more widespread in Finland is the mention of another Southwest Finnish parish, Taivassalo, which forms a similar wordplay with *taivaansali* ("Heaven's Hall"), a synonym for paradise. A corresponding imitation is encountered in Scandinavian variants of the same jest: Ringerike/Himmelrige, Himmerland/Himmerig ("Heaven's Realm"). A similar localization also frequently occurs in the flora and fauna of folklore. In the Scandinavian proverb, sour mountain-ash berries replace the sour grapes of the fox's declaration in the Greek fable. In the song of the Great Oak, Archangel singers have retained this unfamiliar species, but refer to it as a wonder tree, and have even retained the description of the earth beneath it as "liver-colored" (*maksankarvainen*); in its parallel verse, however, it is sometimes described as grain or pine, and the mysterious "liver-colored" earth is often changed to the more comprehensible "berry-strewn" (*marjanvartinen*) earth. The jackal of tropical animal tales is replaced in corresponding European variants with a fox and vice-versa.

Of particular ethnographic interest are adaptations of the kind that are produced by variation in regional custom and belief. Only in Southwest Finland were oxen used in plowing. Therefore, outside of this area the oxen were replaced with a horse, for example, in the song about the bartered virgin and in the tale about the man, the bear and the fox.[1] In the latter, as a reminiscence of the original animal, when the bear is about to eat the man's horse, there appears a cow, promised as a substitute. We find the same relationship between Estonian and Ingermanland variants of the song about the oxen team that is ravaged by a wolf and the new calves that are raised in their place.[2] In Ingermanland, where the plow is used not with two oxen as in Estonia, but rather with one horse, the number two is retained in the song, as is also the bright color of the one animal, which is unusual for a horse. But as a substitute for the two mangled horses, one new horse is bought and, in fact, with the proceeds from a calf born of a second cow at home. In the song about Prudish Marketta,[3] the meal of eggs, pork, and butter is scorned because the respective female animals have had relations with male counterparts. In the northern Karelian areas the prudery is associated with other animals as a result of the restricted distribution of chickens and swine. The virgin does not want to eat the grain of a field plowed with a mare, or sit in a sleigh drawn by a mare, or wear the wool of a ewe. The limited butter production in this song area by its orthodox peoples, who carefully observe all fasts, has caused the butter to change to milk—with a corresponding change of the food to drink. Finnish bear songs were originally sung at the festive eating of bear meat and while carrying the bear skull to a holy tree. Among superstitious Karelian singers who observe religious prohibitions against eating bear meat, the same song is sung when the bear flesh, skinned in the forest, is

---

[1] *Journal de la Société finno-ougrienne*, X; *Commentationes Variae . . . Universitas Helsingforsiensis*, no. 4.

[2] *Mémoires de la Société Finno-ougrienne*, XVI, 146.

[3] *Finnisch-ugrische Forschungen*, XVI, 114.

carried homeward. In spite of its death, they invite the bear to walk along streets between sheds as if the forest were a city. As a result of this pretense, the word for shed (*vaja*, partitive dialect *vajoa*) has occasionally been changed to another that sounds much the same, *vana, vanoa* ("ski track"), or *vako, vakoa* ("furrow"). In addition, the description of the route as "smoothed by swine, trod by shoats, and worn by wives" still points to the original setting of a farmyard. Since, however, Archangel singers do not keep pigs, they have introduced sparrows and titmice into the route's description.

In addition to transformations due to localization we find the same due to temporal adaptations. In the cult of Saint Ägräs (<Gregory) among the Karelians, the double beet plays a role that is later taken over by a double potato.[4] Similarly, in more recent variants of the tale about harvest division, which brings out the contrast between edible parts of plants found above and below the earth, the beet has given way to the potato.[5] Since the Reformation, a minister has frequently been substituted for the superior of the cloister in the farce of the Emperor and the Abbot (FFC No. 42). The answer of the arrogant princess in the fairytale of King Thrushbeard (FFC No. 50), that he is not worthy to loosen her shoelaces, has often been modernized into the reply that he is not worthy of polishing her shoes. The mighty queen of the Goths takes the hero Väinämöinen, as he flounders about in the sea, into her boat, which is rowed by slaves; in a later variation she appears, like a Karelian peasant girl, rowing her own boat. In the song about the elk hunt of the Gothic merchant,[6] the ski pole costs one mark in medieval currency; in modern versions the price has been raised to one hundred marks in order to maintain the relative level of its value.

Besides general modernization of characteristics there are occa-

---

[4] *Ibid.*, XVI, 183.
[5] *Journal de la Société Finno-ougrienne*, VI, 105.
[6] *Finnisch-ugrische Forschungen*, XVI, 132.

sional anachronisms. In a Finnish legend from Scandinavia that deals with a return home at the speed of thought, we find that, as a measure of speed, the usual musket ball is replaced by the more archaic arrow.

An item of folklore is also adapted to the emotional horizon of the carrier or hearer. A teller can confer upon characters in a story his own position in life. Soldiers and sailors especially like to have their comrades appear in fairytales. In the "Finnish Song," translated by Goethe, love's fidelity is assured by the following expression:

> I gladly turn from sumptuous morsels,
> I'll forget the priestly meats.

The last line, which has replaced the original "and avoid the pleasant life," is explained by the fact that the singer was a servant girl in a minister's home.

The influence of the range of experience of the hearer is especially evident in the appearance of the Märchen in the world of children. Lutz Mackensen has shown how envy of parental gifts or even school awards has replaced love-jealousy between two sisters. By making the siblings also of different genders, the contrast is further created between the clever sister and artless brother (FFC No. 49, p. 32). Similarly, the sexual double entendre of many riddles recedes into the background upon its adoption by children.

Adaptation to some particular milieu is further evident in local or temporal designations of wandering legends as well as in the exchange of a few well-known historical names for more traditional ones. In Finnish variants of a legend from Lapland about the return home at the speed of thought, various actual places, persons, and dates are given to certify its authenticity. The concentration of tales around the personality of a popular leader is a familiar phenomenon.

Rhymed forms of folklore can also cause alterations of content.

If words are spoken in incorrect order as a result of a memory lapse or pronounced in a phonetic form with irregular syllable count or length because of dialect variations, the damaged meter again regains its equilibrium through a substitution of words and word forms. Alliteration exerts an obvious influence on the form of unfamiliar names and rarely used words, which through this can attain another interpretation (see page 73). Alliteration has not only determined the choice of words in the composition of rune songs, as we can see most clearly in the use of numbers—*neljä neitta* ("four virgins"), *viisi veljeä* ("five brothers"), *seitsemän setää* ("seven uncles"), *kymmenen kytyä* ("ten brothers-in-law") —but alliteration also plays a significant role in their variations. Its influence even increases so that the normal restriction of alliteration in Finnish rune songs to two words is quite frequently exceeded during temporal transmission and geographic migration of the songs.

The restricted number of initial consonants (ten) in Finnish contributes to this. It lacks no less than six German consonants: b, d, g, f, š, and z.[7] In Finnish prose one must be especially careful not to use alliteration too often or in inappropriate places.

The effort to form end rhymes has also given rise to transformation of content. The original form of the three first lines of an Estonian children's rhyme reads:

> Kits, kile, karja,
> Üle mere metsa,
> Too mulle heina!

> Quickly, little Billy, to the herd,
> Across the lake and into the woods,
> Bring hay to me here!

For the final word of the second line, *metsa*, the word *marja* ("to the berries," "to pick berries") has been substituted for the

---

[7] Medially *d* replaces the older *dh*, to which corresponds *r*, *l*, or nothing at all; *ng* is pronounced as a long *n*.

sake of rhyme; in spite of this substitution, the third line has maintained the meaning of fetching the hay.

In a few Scandinavian variations of the saying concerning the healing of dislocations and sprains, we can detect on one hand the effects of alliteration and on the other of end rhyme. The bridge on which the accident occurs in crossing is not just described as "steep" (*bratte bro*) in keeping with the sense of the story but also, contrarily, "broad" (*brede bro*). Since the word for "joint" (*led*) also means "gate in the fence," it has been used in place of "bridge" because of end rhyme (FFC No. 18, pp. 39, 51):

> Jesus red
> över ett led,
> så steg han ned,
> och vred
> tillbaka i led.

> Jesus rode
> Through a fence gate;
> Then he dismounted
> And twisted his joint.

Further changes are caused by the use of thought rhyme or parallelism in Finnish rune songs. If in a verse pair that expresses the same thought twice in different words and a word from one of the verses is dropped, it must be replaced with a new word; this replacement corresponds just as well either to the parallel word retained in the other verse or to a word that previously had had no parallel. Young Joukahainen offers old Väinämöinen his sister with the following parallel expressions:

> To you I *give* my only sister,
> *Promise* the child of my mother.

The second line has been altered in both of the ways mentioned above. The parallel words "to give" and "to promise" have become either "to loan" (*lainoan*, possibly from *ainoan*, "only") or a synonym of the adjective "only" or "last": *"loan* the child of my mother" or "the *last* child of my mother." The parallel words of a verse pair can also be substituted for each other. If they require a certain syllable count, the shorter words can be extended by means of an inflectional ending; for example, by a diminutive, or even by an expletive. A longer word, if it cannot be shortened as a stem word through elision of an end syllable, is usually replaced with a synonym.

The influence of parallelism in Finnish rune songs can in general throw light on the transformations that are dependent on the laws of thought of traditional materials. Because of this, a brief presentation of various forms of these laws might be instructive.

The words that complement each other in parallel verses are seldom identical. If they are, the form of the word always varies in some way—for example, *poloinen* ("miserable") and *polon alainen* ("subjected to misery").

Most often the parallels are synonyms. The meanings of analogous words have blended together, especially when the nuances have lost their practical application. A graphic representation has replaced the original name after the imagery has been obscured. These and other displacements of meaning have taken place with various words and, in a dissimilar way, within various dialects of the same language. By reciprocal influence of dialects on each other, several designations exist for the same concept. In addition to this, words are also frequently borrowed from foreign languages, which were already available in the native tongue as indigenous tradition or as an earlier borrowing from some other foreign language.

In Ingermanland, dialects are, as a result of diverse migrations, especially intricately blended. The rune song spread over this area like a great flood, from Finland as well as Estonia. In parallel verses we find words that are comparable which also correspond to each other in the various dialects. As a term for "wedding," Finnish *häät* (pl. of *hätä*, "haste") occurs along with Estonian *pulmad* (cf. Finnish *pulma,* "union"). Similarly, the Swedish loan word *paatti* occurs together with the indigenous word *vene* ("boat"). In terms for "street," the Swedish and Russian loan words, *kater* (<*gata*) and *uulitsa,* appear side by side.

A formation serving as an explanation can also serve as a parallel construction, such as "mare" and "mother horse"; "suitor" and "seducer of a virgin"; "liar" and "bearer of worthless information"; and "to write" and "putting words together." Such phrases can correspond to each other. Singers use "brother's wife" and "father's daughter-in-law" as parallel terms for their sisters-in-law.

The law of parity joins words that belong to a common category. The closer their relationship, the more suitable they are as parallels. In a group of four words, it is possible to differentiate between appropriate and inappropriate combinations. In the category of relatives—father, mother, brother, sister—they can correspond in either gender or age level: father/mother, brother/sister; father/brother, sister/mother; but not father/sister, mother/brother. Similarly, in the group of metals, iron may not be parallel with gold and silver, but copper may be parallel with any of them, for it has in common with iron its practical application and with gold and silver its monetary value.

The same item can be included in several categories, according to the divisional system. The moor hen usually belongs to the bird division and to the subcategory of forest fowl. But this subcategory also belongs to the main division of forest animals, so the four-footed fox can correspond to it; or it can belong to the category of wild animals, so that the four-footed hare can also accompany this bird on the dinner table.

Contrast is actually a particular form of parity. Of the seasons, summer corresponds not only to spring and fall, but also to winter. Of parallel verses in which the effect of contrast occurs, the following might be given as an example: "Is there a devil in hell, a God in heaven?" "On Sunday morning, on workday evening"; "Fish dry in the kettle, meat soddens in the soup." The singer complains that her brother has shunned her "as the squirrel a dry spruce, as the caterpillar a fresh pine."

Often a parallel word occurs whose content is neither more nor less inclusive than that of the main word. The following combinations rest on relationships between general and particular: child/ boy, child/girl, tree/oak, produce/carve.

In a similarly purely quantitative relationship, a part for the whole or the reverse, are finger/hand, leaf/book, tree/forest; or song/word, and year/summer. The correspondence of material and product can also be included here: iron/sword, wax/light, and malt/beer. Even concrete and abstract concepts stand in juxtaposition: mind/heart and head/life.

Two concepts can correspond to each other in such a way that the parallel word denotes some characteristic of the main word, as in God/creator and farmer/plowman. One and the same characteristic can be applied in a song as an epithet and as a parallel word, as "gold-maned" for "horse." Not only is the song of Väinämöinen described with the term "humming," but in a parallel verse his singing is also described as "humming."

Epithets that belong to a common noun can be in parallel without expression of the word itself. For the virgin, the rune song has an impressive inventory of terms that can correspond to each other: "Earlier, there were no bound breasts, ringed fingers in battle."

A number of comparisons can cluster around one item; they can be related to the noun itself or to each other. Parallel terms for a young female appear as: daughter, sister, bride, or daughter-in-law. For the singer herself, such terms as bird, fish, flower, berry, or special names for a bird, fish, or plant appear.

In forming a parallel verse the law of contiguity also comes to bear. The frequent sequential order of numbers is often to be explained through arithmetic contiguity: 3/4, 5/6, 9/10, as well as 100/1000, in parallel lines. Parallel words like stone/stump, flint/tinder, and wave/boat are evidence of spatial contiguity.

Temporal contiguity is found in verse pairs like "Did a crow *lay* me like an egg or a magpie *hatch* me out?" Examples of causal contiguity are school/teaching, tongue/word, song/joy, and to be happy/dance.

A parallel verse need not have correspondences with all words of main verses. Often, only a part of the main verse is repeated in parallel expressions. The parallel verse can also offer a new sentence segment or addition to a sentence fragment and in this way not only more richly ornament the thought expressed in the main verse but also advance the content.

The same laws of thought that can be seen in Finnish rune songs also hold true in the variations of all other folkloric tradition.

The law of similarity plays the greatest role in transformation. In the Märchen *The Singing Bone* (FFC No. 49), there were originally two sisters, the elder of whom murdered the younger out of jealousy. Both the murdering and murdered sisters (although less often the former) exchange sex within the generation level:

sister/sister > brother/sister
> sister/brother
> brother/brother

In the same tale we sometimes find as the punisher the mother instead of the father, who belongs to the same age category, or the brother, who belongs to the same gender category, but never the sister. Parents, who are a generalized concept of elder relatives, can also be substituted for the father.

Any kind of similarity in the words can form an avenue for substitution. In the Asiatic version of the Märchen *Animals on the Road*, an eel has taken over the role of the dung, since both cause the exit of the intruder (FFC No. 11, p. 96).

The law of contrasts is seen in the Märchen *The Singing Bone* (FFC No. 49), in which the murderess, instead of being sentenced to death or to another punishment, is forgiven.

The law of arithmetic contiguity can be illustrated by the sequential ordering of Swedish and Finnish variants in the proverb "Better one bird in the hand than ten in the forest" and "Better one hazel hen in the fist [specialization] than nine, or two, on the branch" (*pars pro toto*). The number nine proceeds from the ten-count, the number two from the one-count.

Spatial contiguity is exhibited in the Märchen *The Man Who Could Speak with Animals*, in which birds speaking in the trees are replaced with trees speaking among themselves (FFC No. 15, p. 41). Temporal contiguity of the first and second days of Christmas has caused the connection of the martyr Stephen with the Christ Child in *Stephen's Song*.

An example of causal contiguity can be seen in the Märchen *The Singing Bone* in the change from envy of good fortune in love to envy of beauty (FFC No. 49, p. 31).

Sometimes elements that contrast with their comparisons are used to represent two contrastive units. Various analogues can be found in the riddle about writing: "white soil, black seed"; "white heavens, black stars"; or "white sea, black fish" and so on (FFC No. 26, p. 41).

Frequent and significant transformations of the components of a tradition occur because of the influence of one part of that tradition or some other tradition that has been inserted or where one has served as a model for the other.

In the Märchen *The Man Who Could Speak with Animals*, the rooster's and hen's conversation about food in the story's conclusion has been expanded and often replaces an earlier conversation of the sparrow with her children (FFC No. 15, p. 35).

Good examples of the effect of various elements of a tradition on each other are provided by Goethe's reworking of a Finnish love song that is based on the following form:[8]

---

[8] *Laografia Z*, p. 41.

Would my lover but to me come,
The one I saw before, appear again:
I would shake his hand
Even if there were a snake in his palm.

I would kiss his mouth
Even if it were smeared with wolf's blood;
I would throw myself around his neck,
Even if it had the smell of death.

In this song the wolf, on one hand, has exerted an assimilating influence on the smell of death or spirit of death (*kalma*) in such a way that the latter has been changed to a bear (*karhu*) in more than half of the variants, although not in all song areas. On the other hand, as a result of the spirit of death, the wolf (*susi*) sometimes has been changed into death (*surma*). Furthermore, under the influence of the wolf blood, the snake has made an analogous change to snake fat.

Two variants of the same tradition can borrow traits from each other or exert an assimilative force on each other. In his study of the farce, *The Emperor and the Abbot*, W. Anderson focused attention on the continual contamination of individual variants among themselves. For example, the combination "ruler/miller/herdsman" arose from a blending of the combinations "ruler/clergyman/herdsman" and "ruler/clergyman/miller" (FFC No. 42, p. 265).

The influence of an original version and a later development of that version on each other can be seen in the mixed images of Asiatic and European versions of the Märchen *The Animals on the Road* (FFC No. 11, p. 92).

Alien themes can be more easily influenced by each other the greater the correspondence of their individual characteristics or of their basic pattern. The version of the Märchen *The Singing Bone* (FFC No. 49), which justifies its own name, in which a plant growing from the grave of a murdered person is used to make a musical instrument, arose through the influence of a typologically similar legend in which the misdeed is revealed by blood coming from a bone.

The typologically divergent themes that influence each other usually belong to the same genre of traditions. For a certain number of Estonian song themes, which Kallas has dealt with in his excellent study *The Repetitive Songs of Estonian Folk Poetry,*[9] it is characteristic that a young person who has suffered some ill fortune goes home, tells the parents about the described event in the same terms, and is comforted by them. This pattern has frequently migrated to other songs in which it did not originally occur.

Various groups of the same genre can borrow themes from each other. In this way some of the adventures of the sly fox with the simple bear and those of the sly man with the stupid giant or devil, as well as some jokes that men play on each other, have been interchanged.[10] Such displacements are generated by the Märchen's tendency toward demonomorphism, zoomorphism, and anthropomorphism. A tradition can move from one genre to another and during formal adaptation the contents can be altered. In this way, the Märchen of *The Singing Bone* (FFC No. 49) has in Germanic areas taken on a ballad form, in which the manufacture of the instrument as well as the conclusion are characteristically developed.

Finally, it must be noted that there are often several simultaneous reasons for one alteration. Even spontaneous activity of the imagination in mutation, an urge for variation, cannot be ignored in this regard.

Olrik has illuminated those parts of folklore that are more subject to variation than others.[11] In general the free conclusions of a tale appear to offer the weakest resistance, especially under the in-

[9] *Mémoires de la Société Finno-ougrienne,* XVI.
[10] *Journal de la Société Finno-ougrienne,* VI (1889).
[11] *Grundsaetninger,* p. 88.

fluences of other tales, since this scene is not bracketed between specific elements of the plot. If the beginning has an introduction that extends far back in time, it can easily be exchanged with another. At the conclusion the fixed fate of plot characters can also undergo substantial change.

There are of course traditions, especially in ryhmed form, that begin with a characteristic, striking impression *in medias res* and end with an equally striking, abrupt conclusion. The first verse of a song is often used as a rubric—and not without reason. In the ballad *The Singing Contest*, the beginning lines, in which old Väinämöinen and young Joukahainen stand in opposition, as well as the concluding lines, in which Joukahainen's mother is happy to take the great singer as her son-in-law, stand as firm guideposts between which the narrative elements swing in variation.

There are of course mental footholds everywhere in folksong and tale. Otherwise, in an unstrophed poem or chain tale, a purely mathematical law of variational probabilities would occur in performance: in the first verse or chain element the first possibility for alteration or exchange would occur; in the second, a second; in the third, a third; and so forth, until scarcely the slightest prospect would remain for preservation of the final trait.

A variation, regardless of how it develops, can have a deteriorating effect on the plot. To repair this damage, a later singer or narrator occasionally attempts a new change, which again demands further alteration. When in the *Fortunatus* Märchen[12] the theft of the third magical device, "takes-one-where-he-will-go," is moved by analogy to the princess's house, so that the flight to the island is omitted, places that are easier to reach, like a forest, for example, have begun to replace the island as the site of the magic fruits. Again, a subplot may be invented and affixed to the story to explain the crossing of the water, for example, or the discovery of a boat lying on the beach. In the song about the Bartered Virgin, after the

---

[12] *Mémoires de la Société Finno-ougrienne*, XXV, 120; cf. FFC No. 13, p. 35.

father's *oxen*, cursed to death during plowing, are transformed into one *horse*, the brother's *steed* is frequently changed to a *war boat* to avoid the redundant mention of the horse.[13] In the song about Marketta and her seducer, the rejected child is found in the shavings from a shop's (*porstua*) sweepings. The Swedish loan word quite often occurs in Ingermanland variants with the changed form *porsastie* ("pig path"). This misunderstanding has caused a further change, so that in place of "shavings" (*lastujen*) there is occasionally "sheep path" (*lammastie*). In Estonian versions of the song borrowed by the Finns, *proesas* ("bushes") corresponds to this same word, *porstua*. Parallel with it, *laudistes* or *laudade* ("boards"), phonetically similar to Finnish *lastujen* ("shavings"), occurs, which in turn gives way to *matas* ("turf hill"), which is more suitable to "bushes."[14]

A rather long series of transformations is found in the introduction of the song mentioned above.[15] Prudish Marketta originally went to the herdsmen's huts, but another time designation, "in the summer," occasionally occurs in North Ingermanland. In Central Ingermanland the trip to "the herd huts in the summer" is changed to "berrypicking in the summer" and with substitution of a place-name for a time has been changed to "berrypicking on a mountain." In West Ingermanland the maiden goes to "market mountain," apparently seeking amusement, as she goes "playing on the mountain" in Estonia.

It has been generally accepted everywhere that broad, comprehensive changes occur now and then in which one singer again adds something to the new creations of another. In his *Kalevala* work, Julius Krohn tried to identify such a series of developments arising from neologisms. I covered them even more extensively in my history of the *Kalevala* runes. To be sure, I seldom used the usual

---

[13] *Festschrift für Eugen Mogk* (Halle, 1924), p. 579.
[14] *Finnisch-ugrische Forschungen*, XVI, 121.
[15] *Ibid.*, p. 116.

assumptions of nonextant transition forms but instead relied only on actual, extant variants that were readily available to me in the Finnish rune songs. In spite of that, I recognize that one of the basic errors of my research is the fact that I attributed too great a reliability to the preservative powers of folklore.

According to my early opinion, the creation song of Archangel *Kalevala* singers should have been able to develop, by means of repeated new additions and free variations, from an Estonian song about the origin of the heaven's lights.

In Estonian creation songs, we find (1a) a swallow that in (2a) three bushes lays (3a) three eggs; (4a) upon hatching (5a) the young develop into (6a) heaven's lights.

In Ingermanland the (1a) swallow (2b) on three grassy mounds in the sea lays (3a) three or (3b) only one egg; (4b) in a storm the eggs roll into the sea and (5b) from the eggs arise (6a) the heaven's lights.

In Finnish Karelia, (1b) a duck flies (2c) to the knee of Väinämöinen, which is like a grassy mound, and (3b) lays an egg; (4c) a movement of his knee rolls the egg into the sea and it breaks into six to eight pieces; (5b) from the contents and (5c) the shell of the egg arise (6a) heaven's lights and (6b) heaven and earth.

In Archangel Karelia versions, from the pieces of the smashed egg there often arise (3c) six to seven eggs, and the formation of the world occurs as an utterance by Väinämöinen.

Later I became convinced that two different creation songs were present here—an Estonian one and a Finnish one—which have been combined in Ingermanland. I saw as of even greater import the gradual development of the Sampo cycle. In a legend song about the stormy voyage of Jesus, Peter, and Andrew, the names of heroes from other songs (Väinämöinen, Ilmarinen, Joukahainen) are supposed to have been introduced in place of the saints. The song about the freeing of the sun, in which Väinämöinen replaces

God's Son, is also supposed to be connected with this version. From the union, through internal blending and further additions, the song about the Sampo theft was believed to have developed in Finnish North Karelia. In that very place, too, the song about the Lapp assault on Väinämöinen was supposed to have been modeled after the song about the death of Lemminkäinen, or "the able [God's] son." This patterning, it was assumed, had been used in the Archangel version as an introduction to the Sampo cycle that was assembled there; its conclusion was then patterned after the Sampo theft. The central section about the forging of the Sampo was previously explained by my father as a refashioning of the courtship contests between Väinämöinen and Ilmarinen. Later it became easier to explain it all through the assumption that the Sampo cycle in Archangel was in a well-preserved condition, while in Finnish Karelia it had deteriorated and mixed with other songs.

A truly new creation and creative alteration does not occur in stages but rather in one stroke. It coasts along for some time, however, in the tracks of more mechanical changes. A cohesive chain of fundamental changes is a psychological impossibility in folk literature.

Unique, creative alteration of a tradition through the mouth of the folk also has certain boundaries. Several problems stand in the way of an investigation of them, however. In comparing two widely divergent versions, it would have to be determined that the more complicated one arose from the more simple by development and not the latter from the former by simplification; furthermore, that the development has proceeded from free creation, not through incorporation of other traditions; and finally that they are actually versions of one and the same tradition and not independent creations.

The following two versions of a Finnish song from South and North Karelia apparently fulfill all requirements for an example of creative transformation. They could not be independent of each other; the North Karelian version can be explained as an offshoot of the South Karelian, but not easily vice versa, and the concluding sentiment of the second about the sorrow that leads to the underworld could scarcely be borrowed from another song:

South Karelian version:

My anxiety is of three kinds,
My sorrows are many.
I bind my sorrow on my head
With a band, a silken band.
About my middle I bind my sorrow
With a belt,
And I clasp it with a bronze buckle.
I tread my sorrow beneath my feet
With my heel,
With my shoes, that are of stone,
With the nails, that are of steel.

North Karelian version:

My anxiety is of three kinds;
One I have on my head,
The second beneath my feet,
And the third in my heart.
The sorrow on my head
I would braid with my tresses.
The sorrow beneath my feet
I would bind with shoe-laces.
The sorrow in my heart, however,
Will take me to the underworld
Where hell's worms will devour me
And the death-world's maggots.

Although the image of worms in the underworld also occurs in other contexts and is available to North Karelian singers, its alteration gives evidence of creative production, which affixed a completely new motif to the South Karelian model and at the same time gave it a significantly more intense content.

For the most part, however, it is the mechanical laws of thought and imagination that prevail in the rich variation of oral tradition and upon which we rely above all else as evaluative criteria for different variants.

XII. Criteria

ALTHOUGH WE ARE FAMILIAR with the laws of transformation in oral tradition, the differentiation of a comparatively old version from a relatively younger one by their individual characteristics is by no means easy or simple. The criteria that are available to us for this are rarely unconditionally decisive. More often than not, they offer us only a tentative answer.

The first available criterion for determining a version's precedence is its distribution in numerous transcriptions. A variation that occurs in only one or a very few geographically related examples can in general be viewed as a chance form that was accepted with approbation, or only survived, in a restricted area.

Between two alternatives represented by a significant number of transcriptions, however, statistical quantity is by no means a decisive factor, for this could depend on varying intensity in the field work; more important is the extent of distribution of the geographic areas. In determining geographic distribution, those variants that have been transplanted by means of later colonization or accidental migration may not be taken into account. The possibility must also be considered that a rather small number of widely scattered variants have adopted some one characteristic independently of each other or have altered it in a similar manner. In the Märchen *The Rich Man and His Son-in-Law*, astrology has several times independently associated itself with the motif of prophecy (FFC No. 23, p. 52).

The variants must, however, not be merely counted and categorized according to their regions; they must also be evaluated. With regard to the direction of geographic diffusion of a tradition, greater demonstrative reliability must be attributed to that version which lies nearer the point of origin. A single variant preserved at the birthplace of the item can be of significant importance and may even outweigh all others. The single variant of a song about the Bartered Virgin, transcribed in West Finland and widespread in eastern areas, is of inestimable importance in establishing the basic form; some original traits have been retained only in this form.[1]

The direction of the spread is nonetheless not always readily recognizable; in the case mentioned above, a contrary direction from East Finland to West Finland was first assumed. In addition to this, it cannot be forgotten that at some place far removed from the site of origin a version older than those closer to home may sometimes appear, perhaps distinguished only by a single feature. The song *The Theft of the Sun* wandered from around the Bay of Finland to Ingermanland. According to the song in the area of Oranienbaum, God's son placed the sun, held from its course, on

---

[1] *Festschift Für Eugen Mogk*, p. 578.

a tree, and, to be specific, first on the highest branches, where it shone only on the rich, and then on the lowest, where it shone only on the poor, and then, finally, on the middle, where its rays reached both. In a distant area to the west, an apparently earlier version has been preserved in which the sun first sits on the lower branches and shines only on the rich, then on the higher ones where both the rich and the poor can enjoy its light.

The deleterious effects of time may be weaker in some respects in an area where the folklore item migrated at a later date than in an area where the item arrived earlier. In any case, a regular movement of the characteristics in the direction of diffusion can be recognized, especially when one is not limited to accidentally recorded examples of local versions but rather is supported by its model, as established through a comparison of several variants.

An older manuscript has, in general, claim to greater attention than a later transcription from the same area. However, since the folklore informant cannot always draw materials from his mind with equal facility, it often happens that in a later transcription by his descendents some item accidentally forgotten by him may come to light. From the last rune of the *Kalevala*, Ontrei Malinen from Vuonninen, mentioned before, produced forty-eight verses, but his sons, Jyrki and Vassilei, fifty-two and fifty, respectively. Jyrki's son sang no more than twenty-two verses, of which a part had come from other songs; nevertheless, we encountered through the grandchild a few important verses that the grandfather had accidentally omitted.

The great importance of older literary tale variants was most clearly established by W. Anderson in his investigation of the farce *The Emperor and the Abbot* (FFC No. 42). There are cases where later revisions of an item have prevailed to such an extent that the ur-form has reached us only through a literary document. In other cases, the more original traits have been preserved in oral tradition rather than in the oldest literary variant, which, like all variants, is burdened because it has only been recorded. In his study of the Polyphemus legend in folk tradition, O. Hackman[2] illustrated that the primary folk form upon which the Homerian version was based did not retain the "noone" episode but did preserve a ring episode that is lacking in Homer.

Without rejecting the possibility that the evidence of a single old transcription in regard to some detail can outweigh the evidence of all later transcriptions, the former must, however, be judged in the light of a regional norm, deduced from a substantial number of variants from the same geographic area. Of even greater import is the regional norm that comes from an area close to or even in the home area of the folk tale.

The age of a version is determined not merely by the date of a manuscript. Its occurrence in a colony that is separated from the motherland—like the Finnish colony in the forest region between Sweden and Norway—can, if later transplantation or borrowing from neighboring areas is quite out of the question, suggest the existence of the version before the date of colonization. A single informant is also occasionally found as a carrier of a piece of tradition that is older than the more common forms of its environment. The song style of the famed Arhippa Perttunen in Latvajärvi turns out to be the original one in Archangel Karelia and therefore is often more important than all others. He performs separately songs of Jesus' childhood and death, whereas all other Archangel singers have joined them in such a way that Mary, looking for her child, is directed by the sun, not to the house of God, but to the grave. In certain cases it can be proved, however, that his contemporary, Ontrei Malinen in Vuonninen, who is mentioned above, has better retained the original form.

In a union or blending of two or more folklore items, the traits of the various elements are more vulnerable to change than the independent variants themselves. However, certain details are sometimes better retained in an undisturbed part of a blended

2 *Die Polyphemsage*, p. 221.

version than in a more simple version. In addition to this, we cannot always readily recognize whether we are working with a single, unified creation or a later composite. As has been mentioned, the Sampo Song in Finnish Karelia is performed in two separate songs but in Archangel in only one. Although the originality of the latter version has been proven, the Archangel transcriptions maintain a completely different validity because of the antiquity of individual characteristics.

Segments in an alien environment are very vulnerable to alteration, as are loose fragments. The completeness of the recited characteristics is also evidence for a well-preserved form. Yet a fragment, especially one from the home area of the item or from some earlier date, can be of great value because of the possible originality of the few motifs that it yields.

A variant whose characteristics have in general been well preserved deserves greater attention in certain cases than one that has been corrupted in many details. One must especially observe whether the trait in question has been joined with an older or more recent version of some other trait. In the Märchen *The Two Travelers* (FFC No. 24) the tree is more original than the churchyard as the site of the eavesdropping on the blinded one. It follows from this that those who are overheard were originally birds rather than disembodied demons. In the Märchen *The Magic Writing*,[3] he is to be the ruler who has eaten the wonder bird's head. It can thus immediately be seen from this that in choosing a leader the lowering of a bird on the head is an even more original feature than the lighting of a candle in the hand. Similarly, it can be concluded from the trait of the consumer of the bird's heart attaining the ability to spit gold that even the forfeiture of this talent because of an emetic belongs to the intrinsic motifs of the Märchen. On the other hand, the originality of the dog in the Märchen *The Bremen City Musicians* is in extreme doubt because

[3] *Mémoires de la Société Finno-ougrienne*, XXV, 181, 185; *Finnisch-ugrische Forschungen*, IX, 7.

he has neither a regular place in the night quarters nor a firm occupation in the imaginations of the house's trespassers (FFC No. 11, p. 130).

In the choice between various versions, that one is to be preferred which provides an initial form from which the others could evolve directly or indirectly. In the variants of the Estonian song about the Stolen Horse[4] three different introductions are found, of which one (A) is distributed throughout the whole song area and transcribed in one isolated colony in the seventeenth century; the second (B) belongs exclusively to the Northeast; and the third (C) comes from the Southwest. The evidence offered by geographic and temporal conditions is supported further through comparison of the forms themselves. In the original version (A), the robbed person finds an intoxicating drink (birch sap?) in the forest and falls asleep; in the derivative form he either becomes drunk while sitting in a tavern, without falling asleep, or he falls asleep without being drunk because he is weary of plowing in the fields. In Version A his saddle and hat as well as his horse are stolen; similarly, in Version B the hat is stolen, although it must be kept in mind that the hat was not left outside but taken along into the tavern; and in Version C the saddle is stolen, even though it could not have been used in plowing. In the Asiatic form of the Märchen *The Animals on the Road* (FFC No. 11), it is possible in determining the animal in the water container to choose between a scorpion, a crab, or a centipede. Aarne correctly assumes the scorpion to be original because it could have provided a penetration route into the Märchen by reason of its exterior resemblance to the crab as well as its means of biting, which is like the centipede's (as well as that of the snake, wasp, or ant). As a water creature, the duck is also to be cited in regard to the water container.

A later variation can also be recognized in that it can be ex-

---

[4] *Mémoires de la Société Finno-ougrienne*, XVI, 83–89.

plained through the influence of another feature in the same tradition or even in some other one (Chapter XI).

Differentiating among external constituents in Estonian repetitive songs, O. Kallas[5] complied with the principle that a motif, even if it contributes to the poetic beauty of the song or suits the plot, must be rejected as a later addition if it is essential in another context, that is, if the other song would collapse without it. In two repetitive songs there appears the occupation of a herdsgirl with handwork. In the song *The Lost Herd* it is necessary: the herd is grazing, and the herdsgirl is thus distracted by her work so that she does not notice the disappearance of her animals. Conversely, it matters not in the song about the lost geese whether the herdsgirl has the birds in view or not. The last one does not disappear but rather is frightened by a bird of prey and is scared away; it is therefore unnecessary to have the herdsgirl's attention diverted by her work.

The same criterion is valid in the choice between two parallel motifs of which one is absolutely necessary in another context. In the Märchen *The Rich Man and His Son-in-Law* (FFC No. 23), we find two generally distributed variations with regard to the location where the child is abandoned: on the one hand, the forest or wilderness, and, on the other, the waters. The appearance of the latter in other narratives, for which this form of abandonment is essential and necessary, speaks against its originality.

The folkloristic working hypothesis that every motif originally had its place in one particular song or Märchen has more than trifling practical significance because the hypothesis requires us to consider this possibility in every research project. Even if it turns out that in a few cases two independent forms used precisely the same motif from their inception, this hypothesis has given strong impetus to the effort to establish a firm order in extensive, diverse materials. The possibility of a secondary form for which a common

---

[5] *Ibid.*, XVI, 48, 205.

motif is as essential as it is for its prototype is not to be ignored, however. The medieval *Fortunatus Tale*,[6] which was studied by Aarne, appears to have already absorbed Oriental folklore motifs in its earliest form.

In rhymed folk poetry, purely formal criteria are at our disposal. If the metre demands a particular number of syllables and the syllable count of words in a language has declined through atrophy or elision during the course of time, the relative age of a traditional verse form can be determined by tracing the words back to some older speech form. In *The Speaking of the Stone* (FFC No. 52, p. 69), the Finnish conjurer compares the speech with the agonies of Jesus or of a demonic devourer (Syöjätär). The first line form properly reads in West Finnish with eight syllables and with a substitute for *đ*, which is designated in written form with *d*: Jeesuk/sen sy/(d)änke/ränen.

This verse form also occurs in East Finnish linguistic areas, and, indeed, in the ancient Wermland colony, where *đ* has disappeared. The other verse form is also common. In it the first word is longer by one syllable and would thus be nine syllables long if the two-syllable *sý-än* ("heart") were not pronounced as a monosyllable with the diphthong *yö*: Syöjät/tären syönkä/pynen.

The absence of *đ* as well as the assimilation and contraction of *y-ä* to *yö* are temporally determinable linguistic variations showing the temporal precedence of Christian names in relation to the apparently heathen ones.

Traces of a change are also recognizable if the metre does not permit the same shift for all verses. In Archangel variants of the song *Angling for the Fish-Maiden*, either Väinämöinen or Lemminkäinen appears as the fisherman, with only one single exception when the first person is retained. In spite of this general shift there occurs the line "the fish bit my hook" (*onkeheni*). In only a few transcriptions do we find the expression "his hook" (*onke-*

6 *Ibid.*, XXV, 141.

he[*n*]*sa*), which, however, refers to the subject "fish." To describe the fisherman's gear, *hänen* (genitive of *hän*, "he") would have to be used instead of *onkehensa*, which would cause the eight-syllable verse to be extended to ten (FFC No. 48, p. 15).

Since Estonian has deteriorated much more in historical times than Finnish, metric criteria are of particular value in establishing the basic form of a song in Old Estonian from its many variants.

Because of the very widespread dropping of the initial *h* in this language, the originality of alliteration in the verse can also be determined. In the line *aledaste aine kannel* ("sadly the only [brother's] harp"), the word *aine* (instead of *hella?*) apparently was introduced later, after the alliterative (*h*) *aleda* had lost its consonantal initial sound.

In the Estonian as well as the Finnish rune song, the transgression of the use of two alliterative words arouses suspicion of a secondary influence of alliteration. A line without alliteration can also be the original in certain cases.

Thought rhyme or parallelism in the Finnish-Estonian rune usually has as a consequence a rune consisting of verse pairs. Of course, it is also possible for individual verses per se or a multitude of parallel verses to belong to the basic form of a song. In making decisions, the continuing secondary effect of thought rhyme must not be forgotten.

XIII. Epic Laws

OLRIK'S INVESTIGATION of the epic laws of folk literature[1] that are active in the creation of narrative tradition provides us with additional criteria. In part, the laws are general rules that are universally valid in literary production, that is, unity of plot, concentration, form, and logic. More characteristic for folk literature are skeletal presentation, repetition, and singleness of direction that does not drop back to make up for missing, prerequisite data. Particular attention should be given to the law of stability of the prologue and conclusion, lucidity of content, scenic duality and the

[1] *Zeitschrift für deutsches Altertum und deutsche Literatur*, LI (1909).

number three, and the presence or absence of focal concentration. The law of focal concentration, to take the last item first, merely gives us an external criterion for the location of the most important person of a series. It does not mention the intrinsic reason for the sequence. This position appears to be a varying one, dependent on the position of the character in the plot. In a three-count of the hero's opponents and helpers, the youngest, smallest, and weakest is introduced first; then the oldest, strongest, and largest. The hero himself, however, is the youngest and smallest of three brothers, seemingly also the weakest and even the most stupid. When, in the Finnish legend about the return home at the speed of (1) a bird, (2) a bullet, and (3) a thought, the three sons of the Lapp appear both in a sequence from the youngest to the eldest and vice versa, we must give priority to the first sequence; the opposite, from the eldest to youngest, was perhaps influenced by the relationship of the Märchen hero to his brothers.

The principle of concentration of attention is actually supported within the plot. In a simple enumeration of participants in some undertaking, primary emphasis can be established at the same time, as, for example, is the case in the following Finnish rune:

> There was old Väinämöinen
> And Joukamoinen,
> And the third one, the smith, Ilmarinen.[2]
> Joukamoinen sat at the oar,
> The smith amidships,
> And Väinämöinen held the tiller.

A preference for the number three in oral folklore can be traced to the original ur-form itself. It has, however, also influenced later versions. The law of the number three is preserved in any modification that produces a new form. The Finnish imitator of *The Stephen Song* wanted to append further miracles to that of the res-

---

[2] *Europaeus Handschriften*, no. 91. The order of enumeration is usually Väinämöinen, Ilmarinen, Joukamoinen; in the plot the reverse.

urrection of the roasted chicken and in this way strived for a three-count.

In purely mechanical changes, a secondary two-count can also be detected. In the Singing Contest between Väinämöinen and Joukamoinen, the latter originally offered as a ransom one of his two boats and two horses, of which one is distinguished by its speed, the other by its carrying capacity, and, finally, his only sister (2/2/1). These counts have changed, as mentioned above, not only through simplification of the boats and horses (1/1/1), but also through duplication of the sister (2/2/2). The two-count also changes to a three-count (3/3/3), while the original dualistic expression "take one or the other" (*jompikumpi*) is often retained. Finally, the single sister is sometimes multiplied to three and, of all three good things, the "best" is wagered, as is also the case with *The Bartered Virgin*, which might have served as a model for these changes.

Without any external influence, the primary dual count in the conclusion of the song *The Freeing of the Sun* appears to have changed into a secondary three-count. In the Estonian song about the oxen team that is torn apart by wolves,[3] this is supposed to be compensated for with the rearing of two calves from two cows. Sometimes the number of cows is raised to three, but in spite of this the calves can retain their number two, since this is enough for an ox team. The Märchen three-count of siblings contributed to the addition of a third sister to the two already in the tale *The Singing Bone* (FFC No. 49) in more than two-fifths of its variants. The superfluity of the middle character is made evident in the various ways she is introduced: (1) as an unnecessary assistant of the oldest in the transgression, (2) as a person apart from the plot, and (3) as an unsuccessful dissuader or protector.

As an example of various relationships between two- and three-counts in the same folktale, that of *The Two Wanderers* might be

---

3 *Mémoires de la Société Finno-ougrienne*, XVI, 137.

mentioned. The contrast between the just and unjust naturally suggests the originality of the number two for the main characters; the third person either becomes a dispensable aide or is mentioned as someone who has died before the beginning of the actual plot. The three-count of eavesdropping birds or demons, on the other hand, is apparently primary, since the analogous number of their secrets was originally three, according to Christiansen's determination (FFC No. 24, pp. 30, 64).

The conversation among these three supernatural beings shows that the principle of scenic duality does not offer an absolute criterion. This duality can also occasionally prove to be secondary. A West Finnish exorcism against snakes has the following dramatic form (FFC No. 52, p. 24) :

> Mary said, "The serpent bites!"
> Peter asked, "Did it bleed?"
> Jesus said, "It was at once healed."

From this version with three persons there has developed one with two persons. This latter version simply relates that the serpent bit, and only the question and answer are retained as a dialogue.

Even greater caution must be exercised in deciding the number of persons in a whole narrative than must be exercised in applying the criterion of duality to a scene. Lutz Mackensen attempted to attain an economy of characters in the Märchen *The Singing Bone* (FFC No. 49) through the assumption that the discoverer of the assassin and punisher are the same person—a relative, probably the father of the two sisters. However, he verifies that in 68 percent of the transcriptions there appears a particular discoverer—a shepherd or minstrel—while in only 21 percent the discoverer and punisher, and in 11 percent the finder and assassin are combined. With regard to the father, we find him as the discoverer of the crime in only six variants,[4] and in three of these other persons (a

---

[4] There are independent Greek and southern forms of a stepmother motif that has also influenced a Polish variant.

fellow traveler, a traveling priest, other members of the family) appear along with him. Similarly, I erred in the tale *Ingratitude Is the World's Reward*[5] by considering the third judge to be an original inclusion and the preceding two to be later additions. This assumption has been refuted by more than one variant from an earlier period: the demonstration of the ingratitude of the world necessitates the validating evidence of the two abandoned house pets.

Clearness of content in no way demands an extremely severe limitation of the plot. The marketability of the princess in the Märchen *King Thrushbeard* or the eavesdropping of supernatural beings in *The Two Travelers* (FFC Nos. 50 and 24) may not be omitted as central motifs from the postulated ur-form as Ernst Philippson and Albert Wesselski attempted to do[6] on the basis of the occasional absence of these motifs in a few important variants.

Even an authentically assembled form can again disintegrate to such a degree that the pieces are recognizable as fragments of the amalgamated version but not as representative of an original, independent form. In Scandinavia, the legends *The Throwing of a Knife into a Whirlwind* and *The Return Home at the Speed of a Thought* were joined together. This version, but not the separate adventures, was borrowed by the West Finns. During its further migration to East Finland, the first adventure was omitted again, but distinctive traces remained. Even if it occasionally occurs as an isolated item, its fragmentary nature can be detected by a few allusions to the second adventure.

The principle of stability of prologue and conclusion is not equally valid for all types of folk tradition. In songs, for example, there is a tendency to jump suddenly into the action and break off with a significant situation or impressive declaration. The rune about the Singing Contest between old Väinämöinen and young

---

[5] *Commentationes variae . . . Universitas Helsingforsiensis*, no. 4.
[6] *Märchen des Mittelalters* (Berlin, 1925), p. 306. Cf. *Neuphilologische Mitteilungen* (1925), p. 111.

Joukahainen concludes with the comforting words of the mother of both the loser and the maiden who had been wagered away by him, "I have hoped all my life to have the great singer for my son-in-law." The Finnish depiction of the creation of the world originally ended with Väinämöinen's creative words that heaven, earth, and heaven's three lights should arise from the fragments of the world egg. The simple description of the event must be a later divergence, for it takes place too passively. The corresponding genesis of heaven's lights in an Estonian song has, to be sure, a narrative conclusion; the bird is an active agent in the plot in that it sets the young, who had just hatched from the egg, into the heavens.

The difference between the song and the Märchen with regard to conclusion is especially distinct in the metrical and the prose treatments of *The Singing Bone* theme. Originally, not only a description of the punishing or forgiving of the murderess was a part of the Märchen, but also the revival of the victim. The Nordic ballad version, in contrast, usually ends with the third strum of the harp, which causes the death of the guilty party.

Of the remaining epic laws, logic is one that demands closer examination. Olrik's[7] association of logic with "the drawing into prominence those motifs exerting an influence on the story, especially in the relation to their extent and their relative importance in the plot," also has validity for poetry of a literary age. Unique to folk literature, however, is the nature of its logic, which moves on a different level from the level of external reality. Olrik refers to the "mythic thought process," as explained by Moltke Moe.[8] This is distinctive from the scientific thought process, especially in the belief of the former that all nature is imbued with a soul and that the power of will in the visible world is unlimited.

According to folk interpretation, the Marvelous can be more logical than the Natural in the everyday sense of the word. In the

7 *Grundsaetninger*, p. 71.
8 *Maal og Minne* (1909), p. 1.

Märchen *The Singing Bone* (FFC No. 49), the growing from the grave of a tree into which the soul is transferred is undoubtedly more original than the simple burial of the corpse under a tree. Likewise, for example, in the Märchen *The Questions* (FFC No. 23) how the withering of a fruit tree or the drying up of a spring is to be corrected (the removal of a treasure or a child's corpse buried beneath the tree or the spring) is preferred over what seem to us to be natural corrective measures—that is, digging around the roots or transplanting the trees, in addition to cleaning and deepening the well.

Since even in superstitious representations a certain reality forms the deepest source of inspiration, as Hans Ellekilde has emphasized,[9] the differentiation between the older and the more recent levels of this reality would not be out of the question. A. Lang considered it probable that in the Märchen *Cinderella* a helpful animal was probably more original than the soul of a dead person or a nature spirit. On the other hand, P. Saint-Yves[10] noted that cults of animals, the dead, and nature spirits occur among many primitive peoples at the same time. The possible gradation of their genesis does not provide per se a certain criterion for international Märchen, the Märchen also presupposing a particular development in the interpretation of the supernatural. Nevertheless, the thought that folk tradition in time moves further from and finally deserts the prerequisite that the superstitious be real deserves general attention, as well as more precise study with the aid of other criteria.

Besides the Marvelous, the Normal also possesses a generally accepted demonstrative efficacy. It is apparently a later overstatement that in the Estonian song the pike robs a bathing maiden not only of her adornments but even her clothes, which he could not possibly drag away, not to mention the improper nudity of the girl

---

[9] *Evald Tang Kristensens Æresborg in Danmarks Folkeminder*, no. 28 (1923), p. 59.
[10] *Les contes de Perrault* (Paris, 1923), p. 143.

on her return home.[11] The same thing is true of the servant girl who is given leave during the winter in the Finnish version of the Lazarus theme;[12] her hempen clothes and worn coat have changed in an exaggerated degree to only a shift and sometimes even total nudity. Yet it cannot be overlooked that folk literature is especially fond of the dimension of excess, which is easily transformed into the Marvelous.

In the Märchen *The Magic Ring*,[13] it is depicted as quite natural that the snake surrounded by fire requires a rescuer because it cannot escape from the fire. On the other hand, the addition of snakes and lizards in a few variants of the Finnish legend rune mentioned above, in which a drink of fire and pitch is offered, is unnatural, since they cannot exist in fire.

One must keep in mind that the principle of naturalness also exerts a constant influence in folk literature. If an unnatural representation arises through a misunderstanding or contamination, then it can revert to normality by further change. In the Finnish rune *The Origin of the Dog*, the old blind man Väinölä appears as a result of the affixation of an epic song in a description of being borne in a mother's womb. It was only later that this contradiction in gender was corrected through substitution of an older female character (FFC No. 52, p. 251). In the rune song about Kaukamoinen at the banquet, the spittle of battling boars is used as a fermenting agent in the brewing of beer. Because of a misunderstanding, in Finnish Karelia the terms for "boar," *karja* and *orainen*, have been confused with *kacku* ("bear") and *oroinen* ("stallion"). But since these words no longer fit with each other in terms of their meanings, an attempt has been made in Archangel to remedy the problem by substituting a more fitting, more natural parallel word for one or the other. In this way the bear has often deteriorated to a mare; less often, the stallion has been re-

---

[11] *Mémoires de la Société Finno-ougrienne*, XVI, 275.
[12] *Journal de la Société Finno-ougrienne*, LII, 123–124.
[13] *Mémoires de la Société Finno-ougrienne*, XXV, 40.

placed by a synonym for "bear." In both cases the naturalness of the combination is therefore secondary.

That which is incomprehensible to the informant and his audience should not be confused with the unnatural. Quite the contrary, the peculiarity of a characteristic at the place and time of its transcription offers a certain guarantee that it was already present at the transplantation or transmission of the tradition. Some Finnish cradle songs describe a room made of animal bones, including the skeleton of a cricket, which has no bones. In one single North Finnish variant of this description that has strayed into another context there appears, instead of a cricket (*sirkka*), a hedgehog (*siili*), which lives only in southern Finland and has spread from the southwestern coastal area. Since this animal name could not possibly have been added at the site of transcription, it provides evidence of the original form of the verse line in its southwestern Finnish home. Whenever the name Peter occurs in snake curses among orthodox Karelians in Archangel as Pietari, which migrated from Swedish to western Finnish—and even with the Latin epithet Santta, rather than the form more common to them that was borrowed from the Russian, Petri—the Christian saint cannot be substituted in the Archangel language for a heathen deity.

Lutz Mackensen used the concept of the Natural in an even broader sense. If individual versions of the Märchen diverge at one point, then there remains to be tested which of the various forms would derive most naturally and freely from the plot (FFC No. 49, p. 21). The criterion of naturalness in the progress of a story is dependent, on the one hand, upon the fairly external criterion of consistency, and, on the other hand, upon the more subtle criterion of aesthetic effect. In the frequent attempts to derive the logical Balder legend of Snorri from the confused narrative of Saxo, one must question above all the possibility of such a task.

In his study of the metaphorical language in ancient Finnish folk lyrics, O. Relander tried to separate primary and secondary parallel verses on the basis of the natural or aesthetic correspondence of their expressions with those of the main verses. Among the verse pairs whose metaphors do not correspond harmoniously, we find the following traveler's lament: "My home is in the virgin forest, my hut on the berry stems."[14]

In weighing metaphorical expressions, Relander put particular weight on strength of emotion. When the seducer of his own sister slams his hands together with horror upon recognizing the situation, there are three possible descriptions: "like the two doors of *kalma*" (*kalma* means "corpse," "corpse's spirit," "death"); or "like the two boards of the Kantele instrument"; or, quite simply, "on both sides of his knee." Because of the force of its creative thought and its highly emotional expression, the first variation is chosen as the original.

A more precise descriptive trait is also to be preferred over one that is less descriptive. In the Finnish song about the creation of the world, the diving duck receives the epithet *snora* ("straight") because of its straight flight. From this epithet the less expressive *suuri* ("large") and *sora* ("beautiful") have developed. In the first lines of the Sampo Song, the Lapp, who maintains an enduring hate for Väinämöinen, is called by the characteristic Archangel nickname "slant eyes." In some versions this nickname has been changed to "slant back," which is without motivation. Instead of this, in Finnish Karelia the epithet "lean" appears, from another song about the Lapp, for whom this term is not altogether unsuitable. In the case of the song about the creation of the world, however, the term "slant eyes" is certainly more appropriate.

In one Finnish song the singer gives her sorrow to her horse, since it has a harder skull and firmer bones than she does. This idea, expressed in a couplet, has been expanded further in various parallel lines. The characteristic line "a doubly coarse tooth," whose originality is also attested to by its geographic distribution, is the most suitable of these in the given context.

[14] *Suomi* III (8), 289.

In determining what is natural, as well as harmonious, emotional, and characteristic, there is, however, a subjective factor that can easily tempt one down the wrong path. But this danger can be significantly reduced through a broadened and intensified knowledge of the material in general and through continued efforts in researching individual themes. In any case, a determination of what is natural and aesthetic also demands the support of objective criteria.

But, as we have seen, objective criteria provide us at best only with relative reference points. For this reason as many as possible independent criteria must be applied in more difficult cases to determine the correspondence of their evidence or to consider their disagreement. It is often necessary in doing this to return to the variants themselves or their synopses, in which various traits are presented in their varying arrangements. One can thus test whether the correct criterion has been established in comparing the variation of individual features, or whether possibly an opposite supposition would have been more appropriate in explicating assorted variations.

XIV. The Basic Form

THE BASIC FORM OR ORIGINAL FORM (ur-form) of a tradition that we attempt to re-create by applying all the criteria at our disposal is not an abstract or schematic representation; it is instead a finished creation containing all characteristics belonging to it. It is important, therefore, to establish this form as precisely as possible by means of analytic investigation which advances from a detail-by-detail comparison of the variations with one another.

In comparing variations of a national item of rhymed folklore, even the linguistic expression of each verse can be examined word for word. The standard model of many short international folklore specimens has been determined, almost down to the individual concepts capable of expression in a particular language. The content of *The Riddle of Man* has been completely exhausted by the time designations running parallel to the number of legs (4/3/2 for morning/afternoon/evening) (FFC No. 27, p. 18). Even detailed prose narratives, given sufficient variant material, must be so precisely reconstructed in terms of their content that only stylistic ornamentation is lacking.

This aspiration, as it concerns the Märchen, says A. Forke,[1] should not be stretched too far. Literary criticism helps us very little in recognizing the relative age of forms. It is not possible to say that the better form is always the older, since it could have been created from a simpler, less complete form by means of deliberate alterations.

Olrik[2] has expressed a similar thought in his discussion of the criteria that are present in perfection, that is, with the best internal cohesion and the greatest aesthetic effect. He credits the criterion of the greatest perfection with a certain validity with regard to some types of folk literature: rhymed forms and prose forms that deal with specific ideas. Yet the possibility cannot be ignored that in these creations obscure or fragmentary passages also occur that can be filled in only with other items from folk tradition. In general he is predisposed to accept development from unclear thought to carefully thought-out ideas, especially with regard to the traditional lore of primitive peoples, whose strength certainly does not lie in the area of the carefully conceived.

To be sure, the imperfect design of primitive people's native narratives is incontestable. These constructs, as well as the many regionally restricted legends of cultured peoples, provide us a transitional form between the simple narrative about an event in the world of reality or superstition and an imaginative creation made of the same material but well proportioned and polished. In the

---

[1] *Die indischen Märchen* (1911), p. 39.
[2] *Grundsaetninger*, p. 115.

latter class we include the international Märchen of cultured peoples that have been communicated also to the folk, the so-called natural people. The international tales, like the formulaic and cultivated (in terms of content) songs, belong as a class to a later, higher stage of folk literature. For these narratives, as well as for epic folksongs that stand at a corresponding level, the criterion of perfection in the original composition has up to now proven to be reliable.

Wherever the rhymed form—as is the case with the Finnish rune song—permits under favorable conditions reconstruction of the total structure in the original down to individual traits and expressions, one cannot fail but admire greatly its simple beauty of composition and performance. An authentic piece of folk literature could be compared with a natural flower that can vary manifoldly, depending on the disposition of the soil, moisture, air, and sunlight. These variations of individual specimens are not faults that were present at the moment of creation, such as those of an artificially manufactured flower, but rather later deficiencies, aberrations, and deformities induced by external influences; they do not, however, hinder the knowledge of a perfect basic pattern.

If we compare Finnish rune literature that was still so vital in the Middle Ages with later rural literature constructed by individuals in the old verse metre, the difference is at once apparent. Developing reflection is active not only in the sober contents; even the poetic form, especially in the formation of the parallel verses, has become paltry, shallow, and undeveloped. Thought-rhyme of Finnish rune songs requires such a wealth of imagination and such linguistic vitality that the talent and training given to modern poets is not sufficient to enable them to maintain such a high level of verse for the long passages as was common to old folksongs.

Its inclusion under the rubric "folklore" is not enough to explain the perfection of the strictly rhymed old rune song. The lament—metrically freer, perhaps even older, ornamented with alliteration and thought-rhyme—shows already the weaknesses of improvised literature, and in the more recent, rhymed, one-strophe lyric a lack of taste is frequently exhibited in the adaptation of nonerotic natural images to human eroticism.

In folk literature, as in folk art, there is a question of cultural levels that not only tower above preceding levels but also are well beyond the abilities of those following. Especially in the case of international *Märchen*, it is not only individual narratives, as Olrik has brought out,[3] that exhibit imposing architectonics of which even the art-poet might be envious. Evidence of this is the difficulty of creating artistically a completely new *Märchen* pattern that could be compared favorably with those which already exist.

This does not exclude the possibility that, as has been mentioned above, a gap or faulty section in a tradition could be filled in or improved upon in such a smooth way that the secondary nature of the resultant perfection would be difficult to recognize. J. J. Bédier's[4] skepticism, however, is exaggerated when he suggests that if there exist two equally logical forms of a feature, the primary one cannot be definitely determined. Besides logical consistency and total perfection, we have other internal as well as external criteria at our disposal.

In addition to the prerequisite of an organically unified (so to speak) basic form from which various variants of an international item of folklore emanated, comparative folklore research requires yet another prerequisite: the survival of the original form in the face of all temporal and spatial variations.

The incredible stability of folk narrative has been closely investigated by W. Anderson (FFC No. 42, pp. 399–406). Neither the strength and clarity of the illiterate intellect nor the firm "organic" unity of the Märchen offers him a satisfactory explanation. He refers to the fact that as a rule every narrator hears the tale in question not just once from his predecessors, but rather many times, and not from a single person, but from many people. "The

[3] *Ibid.*, p. 70.
[4] *Les fabliaux* (Paris, 1911), p. 263.

first condition takes care of the gaps and errors that arise from the memory weaknesses of the hearer, as well as the deviations that the narrator himself permits on some single occasion; the second clears up the errors and variations that are characteristic of one or another of his sources." It also happens that when a narrator tells a story that he has heard several times with several deviations on different occasions, his audience will remind him of how he or someone else told the story or episode "correctly" on a previous occasion.

This law of self-correction in folklore is not equally effective in all circumstances, as has been brought out by Anderson.

In folktales every variation from the norm first occurs as a mistake; but a fortunate deviation can, under certain circumstances, especially please the audience and can, with the help of the blending of variants —which otherwise usually leads to a reestablishment of the original form—spread over an entire locale, parish, province, or country; the exception gradually becomes the rule. In this case we are able to speak of the development of a particular local version of the story in question. On occasion (although rarely) it happens that a particularly successful deviation from the ur-form spreads irresistibly further and further and finally overwhelms the general area of distribution of the tale and penetrates all—or nearly all—the tale's variants. After such a drastic revision, the tale norm, which can be deduced through comparison of a sufficient number of modern variants, no longer corresponds with its original form.

In his model investigation of the farce *The Emperor and the Abbot* (FFC No. 42), Anderson showed how only the nineteenth-century norm of this tale could be established on the basis of its oral variants. To be sure, among modern transcriptions from oral tradition isolated representatives of more ancient forms have survived. It would be rather difficult to recognize them as such if literary documents from periods preceding the particular drastic revisions had not been preserved.

Even the age of available literary variants is restricted and very rarely extends back to the actual moment of the genesis of a tradition. The temporal relativity of the basic form, derived from all available variants, cannot therefore be ignored.

Isolated modern examples of an extinct model can still be recognized without the aid of older literary variants. They are found not only in inaccessible corners of the earth, especially on the periphery where in due course an older form (but no younger ones) migrated at a later time, but also (and primarily) in the area to which the folklore item has been exported, as well as in areas through which it moved before the new form developed in some other area, from which it then moved in the usual directions. A traditional form does not diffuse regularly in all directions; it usually persists primarily near paths of commerce and follows the route of cultural drift.

The significance of a fortuitiously preserved West Finnish variant (in contrast to numerous East Finnish examples) has already been emphasized (Chapter XII). It is significant because the entire mass of West Finnish rune songs flowed into East Finland and there underwent change, while not one migrated back in its new form.

Usually, in the study of songs of authenticated West Finnish origin sung by Karelians, however, we do not find any trace of the homeland. We are familiar with them only in the forms that they have obtained in Archangel, Finnish Karelia, and Ingermanland. Fortunately they reached these three song regions by various routes. From their variants we can establish three patterns and through a comparison of these we arrive at a West Finnish basic form that can be detected at various points in various ways. Nonetheless, in all three areas the same lines could have been forgotten.

Frequently we have to be satisfied not only with the temporal relativity of the basic form deduced from variants but also with the spatial relativity. We can determine a North European and even a general European basic form (if its point of diffusion lies outside Europe) without arriving at an ur-form because of the inaccessibility of available materials. This deficiency can be repaired, as mentioned, by means of continued, systematic collection work, especially in India, the probable birthplace of many Märchen.

By procuring new materials, some of the results of continuing research can be modified or even reversed. But what science is totally immune from such an eventuality or is even concerned about it? Only the establishing of alternatives, even if the incorrect one is assumed at first, can aid in solving the problem. Establishing a temporally or spatially restricted pattern for variants of certain regions, from which a particular number of transcriptions is available to us, will provide firm footholds for further investigation of the same form. Similarly, determining a basic form for a few traits will help us discover the base form of the other traits in the same tradition.

In no case do we have cause to resign ourselves to hopeless despair for eternity. Antti Aarne's life work must prove to anyone who does not shun the toil of following Aarne's careful, analytical method in Märchen research that there is the possibility of obtaining significant and enduring results with available materials.

XV. Identity

IN RECONSTRUCTING a basic form, it must further be assumed that the variants being compared all go back to one parent form. However, they could proceed from different primary formations. In collecting folklore variants, a quantity of transcriptions is usually obtained that must under closer scrutiny be set aside or, in doubtful cases, be studied by themselves. In deciding whether they are actual variants of one primary form or not, the criterion of *identity* is decisive. Identity is demonstrated in individual characteristics, in complexes of them (moments, motifs), in combinations of these in episodes, and in the union of the latter into total narratives. We can also determine different levels of identity: from the virtually impossible to the possible, to the probable, to the highly probable, and finally to the absolutely certain.

In establishing identity, the correspondences in secondary characteristics or details that are not essential to the content must be approached with great caution. The identity of an individual characteristic or of a few scattered ones is not sufficient for postulating an actual connection. One concept—the clever fox, fishwife, animal skin, resurrection, etc.—could be independently adopted during the assembling of different tales. To assume generic cohesion there must be a correspondence of at least two essential, mutually associated characteristics.

A moment or motif consisting of necessary elements—feigned death by the sly fox, the fishing of the fishwife, concealment of the animal skin, resurrection by means of an elixir of life, etc.—already suggests a possible common origin of the traditions in which the motif occurs. This assumption is more likely if the one identical moment becomes attached to another, equally identical one. The most dependable combination of two moments is that of connection and dissolution: the feigning of death by the sly fox and the tossing down of the fish from the wagonload onto which the apparently dead fox has been thrown; the bear's fishing with his tail in the hole and the loss of the solidly frozen tail.

The combination is less certain when the two corresponding moments are found only in one part of a tradition that cannot in itself serve as an independent entity. In such a case our attention must be focused on the uniqueness of content.[1]

A. In an Estonian song a maiden who is bathing at the river is robbed by a pike of the jewels that she has removed. Crying, she returns home and is comforted by her parents with a promise of new ones.

B. In a partially corresponding Lettish song, the pike steals a gar-

---

[1] *Mémoires de la Société Finno-ougrienne*, XVI, 280–282.

land from a bathing girl; her brother finds the pike and offers him first one hundred marks, then two hundred marks; but the pike demands the girl herself.

C. In a Russian song a pike robs a girl washing at the river bank of her ring that has fallen into the water; three fishermen are supposed to return it; to the first and second she promises her jewelry, to the third, herself.

D. In a Mordvinian song a girl bathing at the river takes off her finery and is herself abducted by Nogai tribesmen; nothing more is said of the finery that has been left behind.

The pike as a pilferer is such a characteristic feature that a genetically identical fantasy-construct can be assumed for it. Putting aside ornaments while washing is an everyday happening, the mention of which needs no particular impulse from the imagination. The possibility of partial identity of the Estonian, Lettish, and Russian songs is therefore not completely out of the question, while the Mordvinian version appears to have no connection with the others.

The more the essential, mutually combined individual features prove to be identical after comparison of various moments, the more certain one can be in viewing them as variants of one and the same tradition. In doing this, however, one should not include traits that must be considered to be logical extensions or prerequisites of a trait already taken into consideration. So, for example, in the songs above, the washing and the taking of the ornaments collectively constitute for this purpose one single, constituent element. In a ballad about Hansagast in Turku (Åbo), a deceived girl on the beach asks God to send the North Wind to capsize the faithless merchant's ship. Similarly, in a Scandinavian ballad a fiancée who, abandoned on an island, has saved herself by swimming to another shore, asks Christ for wind, which then springs from the north and capsizes the untrue lover's ship.[2] The correspondence between the two songs is limited to one cohesive

[2] *Finnisch-ugrische Forschungen*, XVI, 107.

train of thought—prayer to God, strong wind from the north, and destruction of the ship—which can easily have been independently devised on several occasions during the same Christian era on the shores of the same body of water under the same wind conditions.

In order to establish a certain relationship on the basis of individual features, their correspondence must also be as complete as possible. If we compare, for example, the attempt of the slant-eyed Lapp to shoot the Karelian hero Väinämöinen into the sea with an arrow and the striking of Lemminkäinen into the River of Death by the blind man from Nordheim with a poisonous plant's stalk, we do not find one single completely corresponding trait in the descriptions of the common main plot. They may not therefore be included as variants of the same tradition.

In a complex of individual characteristics they need not be collectively identical; if this were the case, all variations would have to be excluded. Total correspondence of a certain number of traits is sufficient; the remainder need only be similar or somewhat alike. In the example mentioned above, Lapland, lying in the North, and mythic Nordheim are parallel concepts, the sea and the River of Death unite a general conception of water, and the arrow parallels the stalk used as a projectile. But a "slant-eye" does not correspond to a blind man; the dissimilarity of these images renders an interrelationship of the songs unlikely.

Furthermore, it must be taken into account that two independent traditions can take on a common identical characteristic through borrowing from one by the other or even from a third tradition. Instead of being shot into the sea by the Lapp, Väinämöinen, like Lemminkäinen, is, in one variant, knocked into the River of Death by a Nordheim dweller. His being pulled from the river can also be appended, which undoubtedly testifies to the influence of the Lemminkäinen song but does not justify equation of the songs. In the Estonian song about the Great Oak, due to blending with a song about an ash tree, the latter tree is also depicted as growing up to the heavens. In comparing it with Yggdrasil, the ash of

Nordic mythology that grows to the heavens, one must conclude that the chance identity of tree types has no significance. The legends about bleeding bones cannot be considered variants of the Märchen *The Singing Bone* (FFC No. 49) because the object revealing the crime in the latter is originally a musical instrument carved from a tree growing over the grave; the bones from the legend were then substituted for the musical instrument.

Naturally both compared items can adopt their common elements from the same external source, which makes a severe test of identity even more necessary.

In determining whether two traditions belong together, the order of corresponding characteristics, moments, and episodes must also be considered. If we compare the Finnish song about Lemminkäinen's death with the Icelandic Balder myth,[3] we obtain the following sequence of corresponding moments: (1) premonition of death (leaving a bloody brush behind—dream); (2) the one unnoticed fatal plant (*Cicuta virosa*—mistletoe) and the blind marksman; and (3) the fruitless trip to an underworld with a River of Death (mother—Hermodr). Descriptions of the final episode would be too diverse to permit recognition of a common basic form if equivalent similarities in the central section did not suggest it. This is also true of the introduction, where, however, the corresponding descriptions of the premonitions coincide more closely. But the combination of both end portions with the central section confirms the homogeneity of the reports as a whole.

The significance of an identical series comes even more clearly to view in variants of the tale *The Man Who Could Speak with Animals* (FFC No. 15). It is composed of three episodes:

1. Acquisition of the knowledge of animal languages with a prohibition against speaking them

2. A conversation of animals causing his laughter, which arouses the curiosity of his wife

---

[3] *Ibid.*, V, 114.

3. Another conversation of animals, which prevents the man, preparing for his death, from revealing his secret

Each of these episodes can vary not only in terms of its individual characteristics but also in regard to its total content. The man's knowledge of languages is obtained in various ways—not only by freeing a snake or some such creature but also by enjoying a meal of snake meat. The conversation leading to his laughter is conducted by (a) ants or insects, (b) an ox and a donkey, (c) a mare and her foal, or (d) a sparrow and her young, and the remainder of its contents can vary in the same degree. Also, the conversation that serves as a warning takes place between different animals: (a) a ram and a she-goat, (b) a dog and a rooster, or (c) a rooster and a hen. Besides a uniform outline of the Märchen, the homogeneity of the variants is evidenced by the substitution of contents of episodes that occurs in various gradations. From the variants of the second and third episodes we find 2a joined with 3a, 3a (instead of 2a) with 3b, 2b with 3b, 2b with 3c, 2c with 3b, 2c with 3c, and 2d with 3c.

If the number of corresponding characteristics is sufficiently large, the common origin of two items of folklore can be assumed even when these characteristics occur in different orders. We recognize the fact that the Balder legend in Saxo is a variant of the Balder myth in Snorri, not only by means of the common names—Balder, Höther, and Nanna—but also by the following transposed features—premonition in a dream (Balder in the conclusion/Frigg in the introduction), the single fatal weapon (sword/mistletoe), the appearance of the gods (in conflict/in play), the killing of Balder (intentionally by the blind man/unintentionally by the not-blind), the cremation of the corpse in a ship (Gelder's before Balder's death/Balder's).

A genuinely traditional example of thorough permutation of identical traits can be found in a Finnish rune song that apparently owes its development to a Swedish song about St. George's strug-

gle with the dragon. *Sancti Örjans visa*, sung in 1471 at the Battle
of Bunkeberg against the Danes and transcribed later, follows the
well-known St. George legend. The Finnish rune-song goes:

> Let us climb the hill,
> The hill of summer youth;
> Let us fell the tall linden—
> Tall linden, broad linden;
> Let us pull the long bark,
> Long bark, and smooth it too;
> Let us turn the long rope,
> Long rope and also supple,
> With which we will hang the lover (*yrjän*),
> On the way to the gate,
> In the farm-fence corner,
> Where the king passes,
> Goes forth the lord of the realm.
> Sternly the king inquires,
> Asks, the lord of the realm implores,
> "Why is this man bound,
> This mother's son confined?"
> For this reason the man is bound,
> This mother's son is confined:
> He seduced a virgin,
> A young maid he dishonored.
> The poor girl was sentenced
> To the jaws of a monster.
> Even the dragon pitied her,
> Sighed deeply, and drew his breath:
> "I would rather swallow
> This youth with his sword,
> This hero in armor,
> This horse with bridle and saddle,
> Rather than devour the young girl,
> This young-blood maiden.
> Many sons she will bear us,
> Create for us builders of ships,

To serve in Sweden's great war
Against Denmark."

We find here the following traits in common with those of the
Scandinavian legend song: the king, the dragon, the maiden sentenced to death by being devoured, and the lover, whose Finnish
designation (accusative *Yrjän*, nominative *Yrkä*) corresponds with
the Swedish *Örian*. The outfitting of the young man with sword,
armor (*umpirauta*, "enclosing iron") and saddled horse suggests
a knight; his epithet, "mother's son," designates a clergyman, as
it also does in the song about the Finnish Bishop Heinrich. The
accusation of dishonor can perhaps be explained as a misunderstanding of a rejection of the king's daughter, offered in marriage
(by the chaste saint). The dragon's sigh about the war-worthy
sons that could be expected from the bride corresponds to the
king's concern about the loss of possible heirs to his throne. It is
still questionable whether the climbing of the mountain by the
singers is somehow related to the climbing by the king's daughter
on the mountain; the relation is also questionable between the
hanging of the lover by means of a rope and the winding of a
belt around the dragon's neck.

If the identification is based on the sequence of characteristics,
moments, or episodes, then the most perfect possible correspondences must be demanded. And one must avoid deception by so-
called typological similarities.

As Bédier has shown,[4] there are five different narratives of the
type "granted wishes" that because of abuse of the wishes lead to
uselessness or even harm. There is granted:

1. To one person a wish for harm
2. To two persons each one wish for harm
3. To two persons the same possibility, one for good, the other
harm
4. To three persons each a wish for discord and harm

[4] *Les fabliaux*, p. 280.

5. To one married couple three wishes for discord and uselessness

Since the wishes do not once correspond in a satisfactory manner,
they could scarcely be considered variants of one form.

The study of identity also gives us a relative criterion. If two
folklore items consist of too few features, even a total correspondence of them is not sufficient to assert a genetic relationship; the
possibility of independent polygenesis remains. Also, it is not
always easy to recognize whether we have before us two partially
corresponding versions, one formed from the other by free variation, or two independent, primary creations. In parallel verses of
Finnish rune literature there are frequent cases where it is extremely difficult to establish the boundary between a substantially
altered variation and a new creation. In these cases, as has been
already mentioned, it is advisable to separate them (temporarily)
from the main body of data.

In the final decision of doubtful identity, geographic distance
must also be taken into account. With an increase in distance the
possibility of a genetic relationship generally diminishes, with the
obvious exception of colonization.

The vast majority of variants of detailed descriptions, however,
provides sufficient quantities of characteristics corresponding to a
sufficient degree to establish definitely whether their origin is in a
common source.

XVI. Homeland and Migration

ONLY AFTER THE BASIC FORM of an item of folklore has been determined with the greatest possible certainty can one undertake to determine its home. But there have been some early efforts to state hypotheses regarding the actual site of origin of the international Märchen.

The Grimm Brothers believed it coincided with the original ancestral home of the Indo-European tribes. On the basis of the occurrence of the same tales among the Finns and other non-Aryan peoples the first Finnish Märchen expert, E. Rudbäck (birthplace: Salmelainen), expanded the one-sided theory of heredity and suggested that the very homeland of mankind itself was the home of all tales. Then Theodor Benfy came on the scene with his hypothesis that Märchen diffused from India during recorded history. Finally Andrew Lang appeared with his assertion that similar Märchen forms frequently develop in various places at various times as a result of the similar thought processes and imaginations of primitive peoples.

Polygenesis in the most extreme sense, that every variant was composed separately at innumerable sites, is unthinkable. Usually a single origin is assumed for the traditional forms of one ethnic or linguistic group, and a common origin is rejected only in regard to international situations. But even one single independent reoccurrence of such a complicated form, for example, the Cinderella tale, as the result of the general similarity of human fantasy or pure chance is highly unlikely.

The theory of polygenesis is based on the assumption that folkloristic materials are in general the common property of the whole human race, so that every genre could arise among every people and any form of a genre among any particular ethnic group. This assumption does not correspond with the facts.

First, in regard to the international Märchen, it is certainly not international in the sense that it is common to all peoples of the world. It belongs to our old well-known continents and migrated to the New World only with colonization. In the same way, significant sections of Africa and Asia lie outside its true scope, which is apparent from any compilation of variants; this cannot be simply attributed to insufficient field work.

Simple legends based on actual or imagined events are of course to be found everywhere. In the uniformity of primitive life-relationships certain real incidents as well as fantasies are repeated at different locations without their being necessarily a relationship between them, for they lack quantitatively and qualitatively sufficient correspondences. Among the legends of cultured nations there are not a few that are of a very complicated type and occur within restricted geographic or ethnographic boundaries. P. Saint-Yves attempts to support his hypothesis of the polygenesis of this tale (*Les contes de Perrault*, p. 164) theoretically by citing similar primitive rituals from which tales of the Cinderella type could have developed, not just once but even twice or three times.

The same thing is true of notions connected with superstitious customs. As W. Schmidt and W. Koppers have suggested,[1] "It is certainly true of primitive peoples, especially pygmies and pygmoids, that belief in charms, magic in general, appears to be less developed among them than it is among highly developed culturally and economically advanced societies." This corresponds with the fact that the greatest volume of superstitious customs has been encountered among cultured peoples.

It is evident from a purely statistical comparison of Finno-Ugric groups that these customs are cultural determinants. They are least numerous among the most primitive, the East Yakuts in Siberia; and even this minimal number shows a foreign origin. In eastern Russia they are much better represented among Zyrians Christianized in 1400 than among their still partially pagan kindred. These customs occur most abundantly among Hungarians, Estonians, and Finns. Furthermore, in Finland there are noticeably fewer superstitious cures and other forms of black arts among the Greek Orthodox than among their westerly Lutheran, formerly Catholic, neighbors, who stood under the powerful influence of medieval magic.

In the case of verbal magic, international magic incantations that are comparable to migratory Märchen are to be found in the same culture areas with even less diffusion outside their boundaries by means of colonization. Even a comparison of magic procedures among various Finno-Ugric peoples will show us the dependency of set formulae on cultural forces. The East Yakut shaman who puts himself into a trance with a magic drum knows no magic

[1] *Völker und Kulturen I* (*Der Mensch aller Zeiten*, III), p. 472.

formulae. The Lapps, who not long ago made use of the magic drum, have learned isolated modern incantations from their neighbors. Among tribes living in eastern Russia a modest number of prose incantations borrowed from the Russians are found; but in this yet vital heathen culture they play an insignificant role. They have also been adopted by tribes of the Olonets District bordering on Finland. Finland itself has been deluged with a metric magic literature that has its origin in medieval Roman Catholic word-magic (FFC No. 52, pp. 8–12).

The original use of the word for magical purposes, as in earliest attempts at literature in general, was improvisational. Correspondences between various peoples on this level are restricted to the first beginnings of typical expressions and can be explained by means of the similarity of human fantasies or fortuitous coincidence of actual events at different places. The second possibility must also not be neglected in the case of formal, very highly developed, historical songs that belong to a single country and are parallel to each other in only a few of their features. But there are on the other hand international epic songs that are common to various countries although to a far more restricted degree than the Märchen. Polygenesis can scarcely be considered for this literature.

Finally, as regards proverbs and riddles that, individually examined, offer too few consistent characteristics to permit the establishment of firm genetic relationships, cohesive groupings can be delineated, nonetheless, that are unique to cultured nations. Not all peoples have given their life's experiences the crystallized form of the true proverb, which expresses its thought by means of imagery. The posing of riddles is also not a general human activity. W. Thalbitzer has assured us that the Eskimos are not at all familiar with this type of folk literature. A further investigation will be needed to determine how far the area of the riddle coincides with that of the Märchen.

Broadly speaking we can assert that international traditions, with which the comparative folklorist is primarily concerned, are not native to all nations of the world but rather only to cultured societies of the Old World and peoples under their influence. As is the case with all complicated cultural products, it must also be assumed of these that each individual form arose at one particular location.

With this recognition, however, we still have not learned the site of origin for every case. In regard to the greatest volume of tales of wonder, jests, and fables, J. Bédier[2] doubts whether we can *ever* determine their various home areas. Bédier does not extend his skepticism to all forms of folklore. Indeed, in an individual language there is a national folk literature for which the determination of a site of origin lies merely in a choice between various regions within the national territory.

In addition there are international traditions that embrace a relatively narrow circle of nationalities; among Finnish-Estonian rune songs it is valid in most cases to choose between Finnish or Estonian origins.

When we examine rather wide areas like West and East Europe, Asia Minor, and India we detect a certain difference in the permanency of the Märchen. There are Märchen that occur only in one of these areas, indeed in an even more restricted space, and whose homeland is therefore much easier to trace.

But also in regard to those Märchen that appear in virtually all areas of this genre—as is the case with the best-known and most popular ones—we have no reason to avoid a scholarly research for their homeland. We are indeed obligated to assume this task as soon as they are recognized as cultural artifacts.

India can certainly no longer be considered the only home of the Märchen. In my treatment of *The Bear [Wolf] and the Fox*, I isolated a group of animal tales that apparently were formed in the northern part of Europe. Even Benfey made animal tales an exception from his theory because he traced Indian fables back to the

[2] *Les fabliaux*, p. 286.

Greek. I had to defend the Indian origin of a few fables about *The Lion and the Jackal* [*Fox*] against him in the same study.

Aarne's dissertation about magic gifts proved that wonder tales, as for example *The Magic Ring*, could actually have stemmed from India, but, conversely, that others like the *Fortunatus* Märchen migrated from Western Europe during the Middle Ages.[3]

Later, specialized studies have always taken up the question of homeland, and not without success. Benfey's hypothesis about the diffusion of many Märchen from India through the folk process as well as literary routes is no longer vague conjecture but a repeatedly substantiated fact. But in addition to India various other areas of origin have been posited with greater or lesser plausibility.

To be sure, we can trace the route to the home of a tradition only so far as available materials permit us. The conclusion may therefore be a more or less tentative one. Nevertheless we come closer to the sought-after site when we succeed in establishing where the item could *not* have originated, and thereby determine the direction of its movement.

We have one—or more precisely, two—final northern extremities in Finland, which has been influenced by Scandinavia as well as Russia, but which was not a country of passage for tales. Finland is the final refuge for Western as well as Eastern European folklore, but not its cradle. Mackensen (FFC No. 49, p. 96) sees in a Finnish variant from Ingermanland of the Märchen about *Singing Bones* a connecting link from Scandinavia to Russia which is of extraordinary importance for the understanding of Märchen migration. Besides features that are indigenous to the eastern area, in its jealousy and marriage proposal it shows some Nordic influence. In my opinion these are original parts of this Märchen and should be assumed to be part of the basic form of eastern variants; *cf.* the permission for marriage as a prize in some Russian variants.

---

[3] *Mémoires de la Société Finno-ougrienne*, XXV (1908).

A. Ahlstrom[4] assumes that the Swedish Märchen in general immigrated from Denmark. This direction of movement has long been recognized in medieval ballad literature. In turn, Märchen and ballads appear to have come to Denmark from Germany. In Germany the influence of Western Europe is unmistakable; in regard to other currents, that of the Märchen from Southern Europe must also be taken into consideration.

In Russia the Märchen spread chiefly in northerly and easterly directions. The Balkan peninsula formed a reservoir from which not only Western European but also Eastern European Märchen flowed. Here and in Asia Minor the Greeks adopted some Märchen from the Turks, to whom they had been transmitted by the Persians, as E. Cosquin[5] has shown. Specific research will have to investigate to what degree the Caucasus can be viewed as a gateway zone. Probably, like Finland, it was a terminus zone and refuge for two streams of incoming folklore. It can scarcely be considered an emigration region, as Olrik assumes in regard to the legend *The Fettered Monster*.[6]

It is certainly quite likely that there might have been two opposing cultural streams, especially in transit regions. Two counterflowing movements can be weighed against each other in the case in question. But when Bédier does not believe this so likely—indeed, as undemonstrable—his skepticism is once more excessive.[7] His examples (Hungary/Germany, France/Spain) offer no insurmountable problems in the analytical research of an individual Märchen form, if its Oriental and Occidental origin can be generally deduced from the distribution of its variants and variations.

Even the marking of principal routes of migratory traditions promotes further research. In studying Finnish-Estonian rune songs the determination of their migration around the Bay of Finland, from Estonia to Finland as well as from Finland to Estonia, repre-

---

[4] *Om folksagorna* (*Archives des traditions populaires suédoises*, LIV), p. 84.
[5] *Études folkloriques* (Paris, 1922), p. 16.
[6] *Om Ragnarok*, II (Copenhagen, 1914), p. 137.   [7] *Les fabliaux*, p. 223.

sents a significant advance toward answering the question of their homeland. Of course, initially the flow of Estonian songs into the Finnish linguistic area was overestimated quantitatively as well as in regard to the distance it had traveled, just as the influence of Finnish songs in Estonia had also been underestimated. In a few cases the assumed direction of migration had to be reversed, as mentioned before, after later research. The folklorist, like the mathematician, is frequently obliged to test the same chain of thought in a reverse direction in order to validate or disprove by means of a negative postulate the accuracy of his positive line of proof.

There are inundated areas where the culture flow moves only in one direction. The spread of folklore from Germany across Denmark, Sweden, Swedish Finland, and West Finland, to East Finland cannot be contradicted by a possible reverse flow along the same route. Only by way of exception an occasional reversal between two but not more of these areas can be established. The same is true of the diffusion of Märchen from India to Western Europe. A reverse migration along this entire sequence is quite unlikely.

When Lutz Mackensen places the home of the pan-European Märchen *The Singing Bone* in the Flemish area, its occurrence in India confronts him with great difficulties. He has explained this by including India among colonial areas where Märchen can be traced back to European antecedents (FFC No. 49, p. 66). This same hypothesis of the origin of recently transcribed Indian Märchen has been suggested by others too. Because of their great significance their rectitude must be conclusively proved by means of concentrated studies, which have not taken place up to now. In the case mentioned, the contradictory assumption would still have to be tested: the Märchen *The Singing Bone* could have originated in India and reached the Flemish area only at the conclusion of its migration.

The six Indian variants, viewed individually, are, however, dis-

torted in various ways (FFC No. 49; in Mackensen's abbreviation, In1b-In5b, inc.). By comparison of them the primary characteristics of the basic form can be determined. The sister (1-3, 5, k)
is thrown into a well (3, df. 1) shortly before her marriage (1)
because of envy (3, 4). A fiddle (2, 3, k, cf. 5) is prepared from
a bamboo rod growing from the well (2, 3, cf. 1, 4, 5) by a pass-
ing-by finder (1, 2, 3, 5, k). Of course the envy is not depicted as
jealousy, since the sister, sinfully striving for the love of the fiancé
(as finder, 1), has been variously replaced by sisters-in-law, brothers, etc. The fiddle is however played not only before the brothers
(2) but also before the sister (5, k), and it sings to the latter, who
has married a king's son, "the sister went to the water; she became
queen."

In Flemish variants, too, jealousy has been erased; its previous
connection with the Märchen *The Substituted Bride* (V3k) can
possibly be explained by the one-time presence of this basic characteristic in the local version. Envy because of parents' gifts or reward in school suggests the influence of the nursery. It was possible for the contrast between the good and the bad child to be
intensified with a difference of sex; for this reason the envious
sister has usually evolved into a bad brother.

Mackensen places very great weight on the fidelity with which
the concluding characteristics have been preserved. In Flemish
variants the girl, who has been tossed into a well or ditch, is pulled
out alive, and the guilty party is put there in her place. In Indian
variants the murdered girl re-appears from the musical instrument;
in one version the instrument is destroyed for this purpose. This
latter version is wide-spread in Europe too: among the Italians
(J2b), Ukrainians (GU1k), Russians (R16), Poles (PT4, 7b),
Hungarians (U2b), Estonians (Bp1b, cf. 5b), Danes (D16), and
Norwegians (N1h). This version reflects an ancient folk conception of the transferal of the soul from the corpse to a plant growing over it and then into an instrument cut from the wood of the

plant, as well as the liberation of the soul from this encasement by destroying it.

Restricted to Flemish and Walloon variants is the retrieval of the girl from the well or pit, still alive, as well as the substitution there in her place of the guilty party. This nursery version avoids mentioning death, for even he who is punished with death, in the infant mind, lives on in the pit as if in a dark room. One can scarcely speak of this as resurrection through a substitute sacrifice, which might suggest a primitive mythological conceptualization. To be sure, in one French version (F2b) there is a suggestion that the murdering siblings suffer death in the same pit where the corpse is found. When asked what she thinks of this punishment, the dead girl advises how she can be revived and finally asks leniency for the guilty ones. However here too resurrection is not the result of burying the guilty ones but rather of another means.

In reconstructing French variants the more recent pardon must be accounted for, the number of guilty people restricted to one, and the sequence set right again. The disinterred girl is revived by some device and the guilty girl suffers death in the same grave. The Walloon-Flemish version seems to have developed further from this form. French influence in Walloon and Flemish variants can also be discerned at the beginning of the Märchen. The search for the (eternal) flower, which is ubiquitous in France, occurs in Walloon Belgium and occasionally in Flemish regions (V4k, cf. V9b; V7b is told in French within France). The search for the flower is, on one hand, changed in Walloon areas to a search for wood, a gift being promised to the most industrious child, and, on the other hand, to a simple gift of a bouquet for the more modest sister (W1k, 2k); the first version occurs once in the Flemish area, but the second is more general, with a basket substituted for the bouquet or some other object as a gift from the parents or as a school prize. The French term for the flower, *eternelle*, appears unchanged in Wallonia (W2k) as well as in some variations "infernelle," "rose de Saint-Ernelle," "fleur de Sainte Hélène" (W5b,

3b, 3-4k). Among the Flemish we find "Magdalen-flower" (V4k), "a basket [for flowers?] of Sainte Cecile" (V1b), or her crucifix (V6b). The migration of the Märchen in the direction of France/Wallonia/Flanders is apparent.

The resurrection of the corpse appears outside France, where it frequently occurs in a few Russian variants (R2-3b; cf. Rk1) and a few Estonian ones (Bp 6-7b), as well as one Hungarian (U1b). In a comparison with the wide-spread re-appearance from out of the musical instrument this variant cannot claim the advantage of age; at the same time, the originality of the transposition of the guilty person in the watery pit, which has been used to support an alleged Flemish homeland of the Märchen, becomes untenable when considering the resurrection of the dead person.

One should especially note that here I have chosen as an example a thorough study that is worth verification and consequent discussion. I, too, as I have mentioned, have had to reverse some of my statements.

W. Anderson correctly stated (FFC No. 42, p. 408) that the diffusion routes of a tradition correspond to the paths of culture in general in a majority of cases. Such traditions entered European colonies in the newly discovered parts of the world with the first bearers of culture. Here the situation can be adequately described as the influence of a significantly higher people, in terms of culture, on a culturally much lower one. But a chain of exchange of Märchen between Indians, Persians, Turks, Greeks, Bulgarians, Roumanians, Hungarians, Germans, Danes, and Swedes up to the Finns, who have also had connections with the Bulgarians through the transmissions of the Great and Lesser Russians, is by no means a progressive series of the cultural levels of these peoples. The exchange of Märchen in Europe has moved within an area of an already wide-spread culture between culturally equivalent peoples of different nations in geographic order.

A higher culture of the donor society in contrast to that of the recipient is not actually necessary, since as a rule the former is

itself generally passing on migratory materials. The most nationalistic creation of a people, its heroic poetry, seldom spreads across
linguistic boundaries. When it occasionally does, it follows the
general flow of international traditions. Thus the West Finns
freely transfer many originally Scandinavian ballads about knight-
hood and the East Finns some Russian byliny into rune meter. But
Finnish heroic songs, of which the *Kalevala* is composed and
which belong to the most perfect examples of genuine folk poetry,
have not been the object of any attention by the Swedes at their
point of emanation in Southwest Finland or by the Russians at
their final refuge in Archangel. Here the self-awareness of the
cultural transmitter has made him unreceptive to that which could
be offered him by a neighbor under his influence. This also ex-
plains why international traditions that migrated across Scandinavia
and were transmitted by the West Finns to East Finland did not
reach the Russians, and why international materials transmitted by
the Russians spread in the opposite direction to East Finland but
very rarely and sporadically reached West Finland.

It still must be noted that uneducated natives in non-European
colonies usually appropriate only a part of the folk literature
brought by colonists, while European countries in general have
borrowed the entire mass of international traditions from each
other. If we compare Finno-Ugric peoples with each other, we find
no significanct difference in the wealth of different types of folk
knowledge between advanced and backward tribes within a culture. Receptivity, too, is an acquisition and a sign of culture.

That the creation of our folk traditions has demanded a certain
cultural stage, has been repeatedly emphasized. In the two most
prominent emigration regions of our Märchen, India and medieval
Western Europe, one must presume an extraordinary imaginative
life that could create materials attractive for all peoples through
all times. Its Märchen forms must have possessed a particular
migratory impulse that might be compared to that of the Indian
gypsies and West European Crusaders.

XVII. Direction of Diffusion

IN ORDER TO DETERMINE the direction of diffusion of a tradition, we must make use of formal as well as factual criteria.

Variants in dialects of one language, especially in rhymed folklore, often provide linguistic footholds for establishing transmission from one dialect area to another. In the West Finnish magic incantation for sprains, the Lord dismounts from his horse: *ratsa-hilta* (according to modern literary language). The word's usual form in the West Finnish area, *rattahilta*, is phonetically identical to the same declensional case of another word, *ratas*, *rattaha-*, which means "cart." The frequent occurrence of this phonetic form, which in Savo is understood only to mean "from the cart," beside the dialectically corresponding *rahtahilta* ("from the horse"), which occurs in other Savo variants (FFC No. 18, pp. 102, 137), proves its transmission from Tavastland into neighboring Savo.

Such footholds are even more numerous between two closely related languages. In comparing Finnish and Estonian variants of the same songs, linguistic and metric criteria provide a good foundation for determining the mutual relationships among various versions and concomitantly the direction of migration in each case. In regard to the route of migration between Estonia and Finland, it is sometimes a matter of a direct crossing in addition to the generally attested transmission around the Bay of Finland. Finally, the occurrence of the same song in Estonia and Finland can be explained by means of derivation from a common third source. This source can be found in a neighboring area whose cultural influence has reached both nations in question on different paths. A real connection, therefore, is not always simultaneously a direct one.

Besides linguistic indexes, the place-names in songs from Archangel Karelia deny that the songs are autochthonous, because the panorama of the songs does not correspond with the horizon of the singers themselves (FFC No. 53, p. 37). Almost all point over the border to Finland and, indeed to West Finland. The singers have maintained very old geographic names, long faded from memory in West Finland, of which they could not possibly have any knowledge.

The fact that place-names can also serve as indicators in determining the direction of the exchange between two neighbors with totally different languages is illustrated by the common localization of the chief characters in the Märchen *King Thrushbeard* (FFC No. 50, p. 13), studied by E. Phillipson. The humiliated girl is a princess from England in three French variants (RF1-3), as well as in the German (GG4, 9, 15, cf. GG11, Prince from England), one Czech (SCS 2) and one Danish (GD7). In the

French versions, in one of the German variants from East Prussia (GG15), and in the Czech form from southwestern Bohemia the humiliator of the princess appears as a prince or king from France (p. 57). From the French standpoint this relationship between a domestic prince and the princess of a long-antagonistic neighbor is quite reasonable. Among the Germans it is evidence that the Märchen has been borrowed, moving across Germany, on one hand, toward the Czechs and, on the other, to the Danes. In Denmark, England is a more concrete concept to the narrator than it is in East Prussia or southwestern Bohemia; therefore, the contrast of countries here was again made understandable in that the humiliator of the English girl was a native Danish king. The Germans, too, have occasionally adopted a national contrast, suitable to their own views, by changing both localities. In a low-German variant [platt-deutsch] that arose after the era of Friedrich the Great, "Fritz from Prussia" appears opposite an Austrian princess (GG12).

The German proverb "Lead a swine into the Rhine but it is still a swine" has preserved the Rhine location in Sweden. In Finland it has taken on the following form: "Lead a swine to Germany, take the swine from Germany, the swine is still a swine." Without the Germanic model the place-name Saksa ("Germany") in the Finnish version would be beyond our understanding. That the pig is to be washed in Germany is retained in the Estonian parallel: "Lead the swine to Germany, wash it with soap, but the pig returns home and is still a pig."

Similarly, personal names can serve as evidence of the alien origin of folk traditions. In West Finnish variants of the Märchen *The Rich Man and His Son-in-Law* (FFC No. 23) the former often has the same name as in Swedish variants, Pärkkräämäri (< Per krämare), but in East Finnish variants the Russian name Marko Bohatovitsch, "Son of the Rich Man," occurs.

To the formerly mentioned natural historical evidence I might also add here that of the ice in the Märchen *Catching Fish with the*

Tail. The original feature of freezing of the tail in the ice and tearing it off when trying to extract it from the water has been generally retained in Germany, but only in a few French variants, from Lorraine and Burgundy. In the remaining French forms a basket is tied to the tail for safety's sake. In a transcription from the Lorraine "fish" gather loose pieces of the ice in the basket in such a way that this weight causes the tail to be torn off. In another version from Brittany real fish weigh down the basket. In two additional forms from Lyons, Languedoc, and Béarn the sly fox not only attaches the basket but also fills it with stones.[1]

The attaching of the basket to the tail in the fourth section of the Renart novel, while simple fishing with the tail, occurs in older Latin Ysengrimis from North Flanders, showing that the direction was no different in earlier times.

The westward direction of diffusion between Germany and France is further substantiated by its continuation in a southerly direction. In a Sicilian variant the wolf swims far into the sea with a closed pitcher tied to his tail; when he opens it on the advice of the fox, he sinks. In another variant he drowns simply from the exhaustion brought on by swimming.

In establishing the direction of a tradition's flow we must depend primarily on the analytical study of the varying traits in geographic order. If we have before us the norms of the various countries along with individual variations the direction of migration may be obvious. The first observation that I made in arranging French transcriptions of the fox Märchen was the geographic division of variants with the bear or the wolf as the antagonist: the bear in Scandinavian forms of the story and the wolf among the Russians. From this, one can deduce the double immigration of the tale from two directions into Finland.

As has been mentioned before, transformation of a characteristic or a complex of characteristics can form a geographic chain

[1] *Journal de la Société Finno-ougrienne,* VI, 29.

from which can be seen simultaneously the development and diffusion of the materials. Geographic affiliation of traditions along with the relative stability of the basic form is the firm foundation of folklore research.

Naturally the relativity of the material and of our knowledge based on it cannot be overlooked in this regard. In recognizing a borrowed version in one country, Bédier[2] noted that one may not assert that the Märchen itself is adoptive; it may have originated at that very location in a since forgotten form.

But it is not the fortuitous deficiencies and distortions that come into question during a comparison of variants from various countries but rather the stabilized peculiarities that are part and parcel of that area's norm and from which the transcription site could easily be figured out if it were not stated. The assumption of prior extant forms, forgotten at some point, does not at all have, as I have pointed out, universal application, least of all in regard to those traditions associated with one particular culture, traditions that could only have existed in the respective countries at a historically determinable time.

When D. Comparetti[3] remarks that the recognized movement of Kalevala songs from West Finland to East Finland does not preclude an even older migration in the opposite direction and that the penetration of certain songs into the Archangel area was in reality their return home, his hypothesis, supported by no facts whatsoever, becomes quite untenable—if he posits the age of *Kalevala* songs after the year 1000. This same thing is true of international Märchen in most European countries where they scarcely could have existed in the very distant past.

The element of relativity in folklore research is scarcely different from that of any other science whose scope depends upon available materials. Attainable results are therefore no less valuable, because we cannot accomplish everything all at once.

[2] *Les fabliaux*, p. 265.
[3] *Der Kalevala* (Halle, 1892), p. 51.

XVIII. Manner of Diffusion

IF WE COMPARE geographic, horizontal diffusion of traditions with temporal, vertical diffusion by means of inheritance at the same site, we find that the latter is often distributed by means of the former. At various times, very strong movements, usually in the same direction, compass over an intervening area. We can determine within an area the influence of the smaller waves of some folklore specimen even at the point of its origin and its final area of survival. The son of the famed Archangel-Karelian singer Arhippa Perttunen in Latvayärvi did not restrict himself exclusively to his father's song style but was instead also influenced

by the style of a neighboring region. As W. Anderson has emphasized, in Märchen research the "wave theory" must replace the
genealogical theory used in investigating manuscript texts.

This demand is justified, even if one assumes a lost literary
source of the oral variants preserved for us. Only in a case where
those materials have collectively proceeded from one and the same
chapbook could the primary text be reconstructed from them and
manuscript copies. Another method is necessary where oral variants have reached us through several refashionings. The original
text A could, for example, have reached two different narrators.
Its variations B and C would be further spread in forms B^1 and C^2,
these in forms B^{11} and C^{22}, and so on. The oral imitations of first-
hand B and C live no longer than their carriers who could scarcely
repeat them completely unaltered. Nor could they be broadcast
farther spatially than the circle of communication of their carriers,
including occasional trips of some distance. Their authoritative
influence on later variants would be of short duration and narrowly restricted.

This is also valid, without reservation, for the oral ur-form of
traditional folklore. It has long been absent and is represented only
indirectly by contemporary transcriptions or somewhat older variants, ossified in manuscripts, which have undergone the most
diverse transformations. As R. Menéndez Pidal has stated,[1] it is incorrect to speak of the diffusion of the ur-form of a tradition. It is
not this ur-form that is passed on from group to group, that
migrates from country to country, but rather the variations that
eventually develop from it.

Nevertheless it can be recognized in its modern descendants because the self-corrective forces discussed above directly balance out
or destroy the greatest part of these variations. Only a small number of them attain substantial distribution and even a smaller
number then permit additional variations that are in turn redistrib-

[1] "Sobre geografía folklórica," *Revista de Filología Española*, VII (Madrid,
1920), 229–338.

uted. The action of the "waves," to continue the analogy, is as a rule a vertical one, moving up and down at the same point. Wave motion that is caused by an instrinsic flow and actually moves forward is a rare case indeed.

A variation that is restricted to one feature and that is not particularly unusual can frequently occur independently. The Finnish version of the Lazarus theme has been found with the following lines:[2]

Olin orjana Virossa,	I served in Estonia
paimenna pakanan maalla;	As a shepherd in the heathen land;
pahoin palkka maksettihin.	The pay was very poor.

The second line has various alterations, caused by the third:

B. Paimenna pahalla maalla.	As a shepherd in a poor land.
C. Palkalla pakanan maalla.	For pay in the heathen land.
D. Palkalla pahalla maalla.	For pay in a poor land.

They occur together to some degree in the same areas, to some degree in different ones. They are combined independently more than once, but they are not independent in every transcription where they appear. The final, most distorted, form is especially prevalent in Central and West Ingermanland.[3]

Preceding the usual beginning is the introductory verse in several Central Ingermanland variants: "Once upon a time . . ." This could have been borrowed on several occasions from Märchen but, since it occurs within a narrowly limited area, it is more likely the restricted distribution of one single addition. In Finnish Karelia north of the Ladoga Sea as well as in West Ingermanland near Narva the third line is most frequently followed by a parallel line not occurring elsewhere, "the effort of labor was not correctly es-

---

[2] *Journal de la Société Finno-ougrienne*, LII, 120.

[3] The occasional East-Finnish variant *paimenna pajarin maassa* ("as a shepherd in the land of the Boyars") could not have sprung up at a random site but rather only in the vicinity of the Russian Boyar region.

teemed" or "there were scarcely any clothes." These must each have been composed and added once and then both preserved and diffused within each area.

The differentiation of an actual or only apparent association is of the greatest importance in deciding whether individual characteristics developed once or on several occasions. The importance of such a differentiation is illustrated in the investigation of a chain of fox tales, to which belongs also that about fishing with the tail in an ice hole. Above all it is important to establish whether the animal that loses its tail is the short-tailed bear that is native in Scandinavia and Finland, as we might conclude from etiological reference to continuing short-tailedness retained in a Scotch variant despite substitution of a long-tailed wolf.

But, as Gaston Paris has noted,[4] the etiological conclusion might be a secondary addition. As evidence against the originality of the bear he cites primarily the difficulty of explaining the change of the bear to a wolf on three separate occasions. He says that in this case the Scandinavians, who took the Märchen to the Celts in Scotland, the Germans, who transmitted it to the Romans, and the Slavs, who obtained it unchanged from the Scandinavians, could have adopted these changes from each other independently.

Of course it would not be incomprehensible that, if the Märchen developed in North Germany, the wolf version could occur along side the bear version; the former could have migrated to East Europe as well as West Europe (Scotland included) while the latter reached Scandinavia and Finland, as well as the Saxon Siebengebirge, before its disappearance in Germany. But even a triple displacement of the bear by the wolf could easily be explained by the frequent occurrence of the wolf in respective countries and by the influence of Aesop's wolf fables in West Europe.

The attaching on the tail of a basket, tub, or pitcher, which occurs, filled with weights (see above), among the French, with-

---

[4] "Le roman de Renart," *Journal des Savants* (1894–1895).

out weights among the Russians (as well as the Mordvinians), and in one West Finnish variant, is an equally independent threefold addition to the same Märchen. The independence of the latter is witnessed by its peculiarity, that while cooking groats the bear draws water from a well with a bucket tied to his tail, and the weight causes his tail to be pulled off.[5]

With the assumption of the originality of the wolf we have not at all overcome the problem brought forward by Gaston Paris, for to do this we would have to admit the possibility of a double, independent change of the wolf to a bear in Scandinavia and the Siebengebirge. The same change would have to be accounted for in other fox tales among the Russians and even by Marie of France.

The other problem in regard to the same fox Märchen is the origin of their concatenation. In Scandinavia and Finland we find an invariable chain of five adventures: theft of fish by feigning death, misleading one to fish with one's tail, befouling the head with cream, a healthy character permitting himself to be carried by a sick one, and mistaking the foot for the tree root upon eating. The first four frequently appear in Russia, bound to each other in that sequence. The linking of the first three is encountered in the German Palatinate and the last three in the Siebengebirge region. Otherwise only the union of the first and second has been preserved.

This sequence could not have developed independently in two separate areas, in Russia and Scandinavia. Since Finland was not a region of transmission and there is no evidence of a direct contact between Scandinavia and Russia, the most probable explanation is that the cancatenation developed in Germany before the Saxon settlement in the Siebengebirge and then migrated from Germany to Russia as well as to Scandinavia. The single concatenation of the five fox adventures provides the proof demanded by Gaston Paris, that the last three adventures existed during the

[5] *Journal de la Société Finno-ougrienne*, VI, 29, 117–118.

Middle Ages too. Without a doubt the whole series was formed before the animal epic adopted the first two, apparently connected to each other, from oral tradition.[6] This does not of course settle the question of the relationship between the individual episodes and the concatenation nor the question of the independence of North European fox/bear Märchen from South European fox/ wolf fables and even from the Oriental jackal Märchen.[7]

The choice between a single alteration and repeated similar changes must be dealt with on the same basis of sufficient correspondences as the choice between single or multiple original creations.

The frequent relapse to the older form and the repeated occurrence of the same variation reduces to a significant degree the possible number of variations that otherwise would expand step by step in a geometric progression. Every geographic area has at some point in time a norm-version that is maintained constantly and comprehensively in regard to both its secondary and primary features. As mentioned, there are spatial and temporal versions that are passed on and spread under the social control of the occasional variations of a particular narrator in order to yield to another new version at a later time or in a remote area.

The frequent unions and blendings of various traditions from which often only individual episodes or motifs are taken have given rise to the view that these sections and fragments lead a separate existence and beget kaleidoscopic forms in random combinations. We can most clearly recognize this in the expansion of individual couplets of a rune song outside its area in an alien context.

The Estonians as well as the Finns have composed a particular

---

[6] G. Paris wrote to me September 17, 1895, "I appreciate your arguments in at least a part of your thesis and I am keeping your letter in order to use it in case the question of animal tales and the Roman du Renard recurs."

[7] In regard, for example, to the foot/root episode, which in India transpires between the jackal and crocodile (*Journal de la Société Finno-ougrienne*, VI, 63).

song about a giant ox. In the Estonian harvest song the singer praises the innkeeper for the difficult slaughter of the ox, whose horns are one hundred fathoms long and whose back is one thousand spans broad. The Finnish song tells about the laborious killing of an ox so big that a swallow takes a day to fly between the horns and a squirrel needs a month to run the length of his spine. This song entered northeastern Estonia from Ingermanland and mixed at various times with Estonian versions until finally only the description of his size remains in the Finnish version. Within and along with the Estonian song it migrated further to the west to Ösel. On the other hand, the Estonian song has conversely influenced the Finnish song in West Ingermanland. Its description of the ox's size has spread with the Finnish song eastward toward Ingermanland; in this way the Estonian description of his back (*turja*) has been changed to the phonetically similar Finnish word for mouth (*turpa*).

The description in an Estonian courting song about the rowing of the old people who shake their heads without moving the ship and the young ones whose oars bend and drive the ship to its goal has in Ingermanland caused a combination of this song with the Finnish song about the voyage of the Lord and migrated in this form to Finnish East Karelia. Here it was accepted into a further combination with Väinämöinen's voyage and then in its new form penetrated the Archangel area. Yet one cannot consider an independent existence for this quatrain.

In a like manner motifs and episodes have moved from one Märchen to another and then migrated farther in a new form until they have entered a new union and then moved on a new path. The only thing that can spread independently is something that can be recited as a whole. Amputated fragments appear during the deterioration of folklore but they do not spread farther.

XIX. Time of Origin

INSOFAR AS FOLKLORE is a culture product, its time of origin must be determinable. Its age cannot be placed in some remote past without further examination. In historical research one proceeds from the dating of the oldest documents and penetrates ever deeper into the past, tracing with great care structural as well as content indexes. This method is also the only correct one in folklore research.

It is obvious that folk literature in rhymed form cannot be older than the meter with the linguistic level assumed for it. Foreign words and concepts, too, that were unknown before a cer-

tain time, provided they were not added later, give some orienta-
tion for determining age of a tradition. In this process one must
not permit himself to be deceived by the possibility that the underlying events are older than they are. J. Bédier has demonstrated
that French heroic songs are significantly younger than the historical figures that are sung about. A similar case is to be assumed
in Finnish rune songs that must assume a historical foundation.
Such an assumption is supported particularly by Low German culture words, transmitted through Sweden.

The Lett researcher P. Schmidt writes:[1]

I see that Finnish and Latvian folksongs, and probably Estonian and
Lithuanian too, are to some degree similar and therefore their beginnings and ages cannot be too different. Some reminiscences, the names
of heroes, and their feats could extend back into prehistoric times but
the living conditions sung about and linguistic chronologies barely go
back further than the thirteenth century. One language cannot exist for
a thousand or more years, and if we accept that, then Märchen are not
really old at all. But if old songs are linguistically changed and adapted in their contents to new living conditions, then they are no longer
the same songs they were formerly.

In regard to international prose narratives, their literary adaptations lead us only to the most recent times, the *terminus a quem*,
which, to be sure, in some cases apparently lies far in the past. But
even the earliest time limits, the *terminus a quo*, can be determined
from the content of a Märchen form, after its basic form has been
established with the help of known cultural-historical facts.

The age of the Märchen *The Magic Ring* is determined by the
appearance of the tame cat.[2] In addition to this the farmyard
rooster is encountered in the European Märchen *The Animals on
the Road* (FFC No. 11). Knowledge of writing is presumed by
the deceptive letter in the Märchen *The Rich Man and His Son-*

[1] May 22, 1924.
[2] *Mémoires de la Société Finno-ougrienne*, XXV (1908).

in-Law (FFC No. 23), as is also the case with the magic writing under the wings in the Märchen *The Magic Bird*.[3]

The animals in *The Animals on the Road* are understood to be representatives of different crafts, which indicates advanced community development. In the *Fortunatus* Märchen we are transported to a land with soldiers and doctors who belong demonstrably to the original form of the tale.[4]

Nor is it any more possible for a Märchen to develop at any random time than at a random place. During my collection trips, even unsuccessful efforts to perform a newly composed work of phantasy were seldom encountered.

Uniquely European Märchen belong primarily to the Middle Ages. It is to be hoped that, in the future, renewed research will answer the question of India's creative era more precisely than has been the case up to now. The remnants of old Egyptian Märchen suggest an even earlier period of activity.

One can also establish the age of sequential variations of a Märchen, as W. Anderson has brilliantly done in his study of *The Emperor and the Abbot* (FFC No. 42). The scientific significance of our efforts to bring temporal order into folklore materials is not hindered by the fact that we must also be satisfied with relative results in our datings.

With a ruthless critique that pushes to the side everything that could possibly stem from a recent date, we can penetrate to the most distant past. After this has been recognized and investigated, those materials unjustly attributed to a recent era can again be restored to their rightful places. Only by means of the severest separation of all even minimally doubtful materials were the most ancient Finnish rune songs, which actually turned out to be heroic lays, brought to light. After the precise determination of their existence and individuality, the discovery of contemporary songs among the previously separated materials was an easy task.

[3] *Ibid.*
[4] *Ibid.*

XX. Foundations

THE FINAL TASK of folklore research is the study of the culture medium from which various folk traditions have sprouted. The scholar's interest has from the beginning been more excited by the questions of how folk traditions develop and why, than where and when. It is natural that one would like to have a prior idea of the goal one is attempting to reach. On the other hand, in no science is there a direct highway to truth. Not only is indefatigable analytic-comparative labor with minute detail required to find the correct path and approach the final goal, but also more or less lucky attempts in the right directions. I must repeat that only after the identification of its basic form is tradition useful in studying its organization, its individual elements, and their origin. But so much has already been accomplished in individual projects that general viewpoints for discussion and further research can be established.

First we must consider the new creations that arise as a result of the transformation, imitation, and union of already extant traditions within the same genre.

An example of creative transformation can be found in the Finnish song that developed from elements of the St. George legend by means of a total alteration of its traits (Chapter XV). The European version of the Märchen *The Animals on the Road* is an example of creative imitation modeled from an actual Asiatic prototype (FFC No. 11; Grimm Nos. 27 and 10). Creative union is represented by the widely distributed Finnish legend about the man who throws his knife into a whirlwind, then comes upon the Lapp who has been wounded in the whirlwind, is sent home by this personage at the speed of thought, and must sacrifice his black oxen as fee for his passage. This was compiled in Scandinavia from various independent legends into a cohesive unity, and then, as a polished entity, it migrated to Finland. In its spread from West Finland the introduction was separated again from the main body of the tale, but not without leaving behind distinct traces; it, too, has been occasionally transcribed in Finland as an apparently detached fragment.[1]

Aarne's investigation of the *Fortunatus* Märchen[2] has shown how individual constituents of Oriental Märchen can be used in the formation of medieval, West European tales.

Various genres of folklore can also stand in a genetic relationship. R. Petsch is of the opinion that "the riddle is unmistakably close to the proverb because it directs itself particularly to the hear-

[1] This research, conducted in the Norwegian Institute for Comparative Culture Research, will appear in the FFC series (*Cf.* Archer Taylor, *The Black Ox*, FFC No. 70—Translator.)

[2] *Mémoires de la Société Finno-ougrienne*, XXV (1908), 140.

er's understanding, and it has borrowed from the proverb a series
of structural elements: above all the tendency toward contrastive
sharpening, animation of inanimate objects, and metaphorical conceptualization of its objects."[3] Of course the proverb appears to be
older than the riddle, but both can be traced independently back to
the use of imagery in speech.

Furthermore, Petsch says that a new, humorous world of struc-
tures developed from serious magical incantations. The riddle
about the featherless bird, which he uses as an example, has been
more closely examined by Aarne, and he concluded that if the one
arose from the other, the riddle apparently existed earlier and gave
rise to the magic incantation (FFC No. 28, p. 47). We can con-
firm indubitable evolution of a riddle into a magic saying in some
Finnish origin runes (FFC No. 52, pp. 34, 259).

Occasionally chain songs have developed from several riddles
and their answers. Similar sequences appear in diverse question
poems—even philosophical and ritual ones—and presume the use
of individual riddles as pure plays of fantasy.

In Finland didactic rune songs arose through the linking of
various proverbs, which have occasionally been put into the mouth
of old Väinämöinen, as well as through the repetition of the same
thought with variations of metaphoric illustrations.

> It is better to sip water
> From birchbark in one's own land,
> From a scoop of husks,
> Than drink beer from a silver mug
> In a distant foreign land.
>
> It is better to sleep
> On the washroom stove in one's own land,
> On the stone rubble,
> Than to lounge in a featherbed
> In a distant foreign land.

[3] *Das deutsche Volksrätsel* (Strassburg, 1917), pp. 12, 16.

> It is better to tramp
> Across the great moors in one's own land,
> To splash in a moldy swamp,
> Than stride a paved street
> In a distant foreign land.

It is hard to find something relative to folk belief in riddles without presuming concealed thoughts in them and arbitrarily interpreting these thoughts. In proverbs, on the other hand, superstitious images frequently retain a crystallized form that is more easily impressed on memory.

Rhymed literature is, in relation to unrhymed, generally the receiving element. If we encounter the same tale in the form of a widely distributed Märchen and a song restricted to a narrower region, then without reservation the first must be granted the benefit of seniority. Of course a song can sometimes lose its rhymed form and re-appear as a prose narrative, but this does not then diffuse more widely. By way of exception one Märchen variant also borrowed a trait from a corresponding song sung in the same area. As Aarne has shown,[4] the West Ingermanland version of the song *Freeing the Sun* has borrowed from the tale *The Magic Flight* the trait of hurling objects over one's shoulder. From the song, in turn, a yarn knot with which the sun's guard was originally mesmerized has been attached to a Märchen variant from the same area about throwing things behind one in flight.

When a number of Lapp, Finnish, and Estonian legends correspond to the Eddic poem about the regaining of the thunder god's hammer, this could be viewed as a prose formation of a Thor-song in view of Scandinavian influences. Since, however, this same story occurs in two deteriorated but mutually complementary Roumanian legends, the only possible explanation is that we are dealing with a general European prose tradition that first

---

[4] *Suomi* IV (18), 79–82.

acquired its poetic form in the Eddic poem and then assumed uniquely Nordic deity names.[5]

A union of prose and verse even occurs now and then. Their relationship to each other can vary. The tale can merely serve as explication, as is the case in the lullaby of the unfaithful wife, who uses it to warn her lover of the presence of her husband. In the Lenora legend one can pose the question whether the little verse about the brightly shining moon and fast-riding death forms the firm nucleus about which the variations of the narrative weave their colorful fabric. In the Märchen *The Singing Bone* the song of the betraying instrument adheres very closely to the story's variations and therefore has been improvised anew, not only in each language but indeed in every variant.

The oldest magic formulae are formed in connection with superstitious customs. After belief in a saying's efficacy has developed into belief in the strength of the correctly recited formula and the contents that must convince the spirits, it has again and again taken advantage of rhymed form, which provides a support for the memory, and become connected not only with lyric but also with epic poetry. The Christian legend supplied the narrative substance for the European magic incantations. In Finland a particular kind of magic origin rune has developed from etiological legends; it also annexed elements from heroic songs (FFC No. 52).

Of course superstitious notions are the basis of superstitious customs. The prohibition against cutting one's nails on a holiday is based on the belief that the spirits are in motion on holidays and can take control of a man if they can only obtain one small part of him (*pars pro toto*). The explanations of modern commentators, however, can include later notions, whose variations are not dependent on ethnographical hereditary relationships but rather on geographic proximity. Thus, three different groups of explanations are associated with the prohibitions against cutting nails among

---

[5] Kaarle Krohn, *Skandinavisk Mytologi* (Helsinki, 1922), pp. 202–207.

various Finno-Ugric peoples and their immediate neighbors, as is apparent from A. Hämäläinen's Finnish essay on the substance of the human body in Finno-Ugric folk belief. Common to the Finns, Lapps, and Scandinavians is the notion that the devil builds a ship with carelessly discarded nails and that with the ship he fetches souls at death or at the Last Judgment. The Estonians along with the Latvians, Lithuanians, and White Russians believe that Satan prepares a hat from nail cuttings, which makes him invisible and therefore gives him freer opportunity to mislead man. Like the Great Russians, the Mordvinians, Cheremis, Voguls, and East Jakuts believe that man must preserve his nails so that he will be able, upon his death, to climb a steep, glasslike mountain.

A superstitious belief can also be told in the form of a legend, an illustration of what happens to this person or that. The narrated exemplary tale is usually secondary in respect to the superstitious belief contained in the tale; but the fable, in respect to the moral that contains the basic thought of the fable, is most often primary literature. The Greek fable about the fox that finds out the grapes are sour has given rise to a Swedish proverb in which the grapes—unknown to the Swedes—were replaced by the ever-sour mountain-ash berry. Priority is to be granted the fable even in the case where it is preserved in its apparent home only as a proverb and outside of it only in altered variants, as is apparent from my investigation of the ancient Greek fable, "The fox knows much, but the hedgehog has a mighty agent."[6]

It is obvious that the Märchen has drawn abundantly from superstition. But a firm differentiation must be made between the superstitious content of a Märchen's indigenous basic form and later additions from the superstitious notions and customs in the variants of a transition region. As Aarne has stated (FFC No. 23, p. 194), this differentiation is of particular importance for the use of Märchen as an auxiliary in mythological and sociological re-

[6] *Am Urquell* (1892), p. 177.

search. Elements that later penetrated into the area's regional tales from local superstitions are evidence of course of the notions of this area at the time of the item's origin but not at all of those of another area or earlier times. The original characteristics of an international Märchen provide in turn no evidence of the indigenous notions of any region other than its own.

In addition, in the case of the well-developed, international Märchen, we must distinguish between its direct and indirect association with superstition. A few magical devices and tricks have frequently been borrowed directly from superstitious beliefs and added as later ameliorations to the Märchen. The original existence of superstitious notions and customs in Märchen presumes the earlier extant, legendary tales about contacts with the supernatural world. Among the Kiwai-Papuans, G. Landtman, who recognized this relationship, came upon some of our migratory Märchen adventures told as actual happenings. The following story, told as truth, corresponds to our Märchen about a prince's bride who is thrown into the water and the girl who is substituted in her place (Grimm No. 135):[7] A mother sought for her son's bride a maiden whom his arm band would fit (like Cinderella and the shoe), and she takes her home in a canoe. In spite of the girl's parents' warning she sleeps one night en route. An evil woman robs the girl of her clothes, puts her into a hollowed root, and throws it into the water. But then the woman is brought to the bridegroom in place of the bride. During the night the root floats to the beach, and the song of the trapped girl is heard in it; in this way the true situation comes to light.

Even if this tale were not indigenous, it scarcely could have immigrated as a Märchen and then changed to a legend. It could have sprung directly from a legend that represented the belief in a substitute bride and that served as the basis for the Märchen at its point of origin.

[7] The Folk-Tales of the Kiwai-Papuans (Acta Soc. Sc. Fenn.) XLVII, no. 150.

From the variants of the Märchen *The Singing Bone* (FFC No. 49) we differentiate the legend *The Bleeding Bone*, which did not expand into a Märchen but was merely connected with a tale. The tale about a musical instrument prepared from a plant growing over a grave probably has its foundation in a legend and evolved into a ballad.

P. Saint-Yves[8] tried to demonstrate that a Märchen's basic outline could develop in conscious relationship to a particular complex of superstitious customs (ad hoc, as it were) and thus be explained as a commentary on a primitive ritual; his reasoning, however, in no way proves the case. Suspicions are caused not only by his operating with individual variants and their frequently fortuitous characteristics but, above all, by the fact that the liturgies from which the Märchen is said to have developed are not available but instead must be inferred from the Märchen itself.

This same observation is true of attempts to derive the Märchen from the so-called nature myths. Personification of natural forces is age-old. But it is questionable whether the cult of nature gods is present at an earlier stage than the cult of agriculture, which is dependent on the influences of the sun, storm, and fertility. Above all, however, it is important to test to what degree the course of natural events has given rise to detailed narrative.

In the more precise examination of Icelandic Eddic myths it is revealed that they are nothing more than profane narratives bearing mythological names, occurring elsewhere as Märchen, legends, farces, or anecdotes. I have not found a single sure example of a true nature myth among either the Scandinavians or the Finns. In Latvian songs about the marriage of the Sun and Moon, these heavenly bodies are purely poetic designations for the bride and groom, as is the case of the thunder-god as the bride's suitor.[9]

Of course etiological explanations of natural objects and events are also designated as myths. They can sometimes be transformed

[8] *Les contes de Perrault*, p. 395.
[9] Kaarle Krohn, *Skandinavisk Mytologi*, pp. 64, 317.

into a Märchen free of etiological conclusions, as is possibly the case with the tale about the origin of the bear's short tail (lost in fishing with it through the ice) when this tale was adapted to the fox adventures. On the other hand, on some occasions an etiological conclusion is appended to a Märchen so that it seemingly has the form of an origin myth.

The expression "myth" can be dispensed with in this instance and we can use the simpler "origin legend," since the latter, just as other legends, is distinguished from the Märchen by its claim to credibility. This distinction is the essential one between the legend and the Märchen. By blending various legends a far more complex story can be formed, which does not stand behind the true Märchen in its structure but does not lose its own character through this blending. A legend can also spread like the wandering Märchen. Conversely, a Märchen can take on local and historical color without departing from the general entertaining tone.

Legendary narratives as well as superstitious customs presume, on the one hand, belief in an inner, invisible world and a causal association between it and the external, visible world, but presumes, on the other hand, actual experiences in the external world, too. The latter consist of events and observations of nature and human experience. Folk belief is nurtured by the bizarre in the external world and by spiritual processes in the unconscious state. In the dream and in the ecstatic state the human psyche feels free not only of the body but also of the boundaries of space and time, and in hallucination man's environment is filled with fantastic beings.

It is apparent that hallucination has given the legend about nature spirits a certain coloring. The forest spirit wears green clothes, the water spirit blue; under the clothes of the first is the tail of a forest creature or a domestic animal that frequents the forest, under those of the latter a fish tail. But note that the respective hallucinations only occur among peoples where the corresponding superstitious notions also exist. The forest maiden peculiar to the Scandinavians and West Finns does not appear in any East Finn's visions. The same hallucinatory form cannot arise in two different societies, civilized or primitive.

The content of dreams is also dependent on the imaginative scope of the dreamer. Our international Märchen cannot, therefore, have emanated from the dreams of just any primitive man, for they contain mental images that belong to a particular, relatively advanced cultural level. Besides, they stand only in an individual relationship with dreams that must have first evoked concepts of belief and legendlike narratives.

Actual experiences in legends and customs can be separated from superstitious notions by means of the regional limitations of the former. It cannot be accidental that actual weather observations do not once agree for a single country while certain precepts for planting associated with All Saints' Day in South Germany and Finland are the same (FFC No. 31, p. 38).

If we cannot establish foreign parallels for Finnish heroic songs with complete evidence, in spite of our sincerest efforts, then the conclusion that they developed from the foundation of actual, historical events, is not unjustified. These too can recur accidentally, but only in sporadic cases. In general, the unique quality of a legendary tale speaks for its basis in reality, which of course superstition and the need for explanatory causes can elaborate.

The reality of a tradition can be of a typical kind, as it is in Märchen. Here we find the most diverse relationships between members of a family—between parents and children (not forgetting the stepmother), among siblings, and between man and woman (before as well as after marriage)—as well as other relationships that exhibit advanced social development, as for example those between master and servant, ruler and thief. The contrast between domesticated animals, which have developed in relatively recent historical times, and wild animals points to certain cultural conditions. The relationship between the fox and the bear has a parallel in the contrast between the weak but clever boy and the strong but stupid giant—which perhaps reflects the conflict between two races

or cultural levels. The Märchen's broad and prevalent encouragement of cleverness is particularly characteristic of the realistic element of the Märchen's world view. Internal and external observations and experiences provided material for folk traditions; they
have been further reworked by the human imagination. The development of the polished narrative of a local event into an international migratory tale is the result of the imagination's continued
activity.

The union of a simple idea, corresponding to experience, with a
poetic image in the proverb presumes the use of metaphorical expressions in everyday speech. A similar combination of an image,
usually borrowed from nature, with a thought, usually of erotic
content, can be found in the wide-spread one-strophe lyric. Here
we find a powerfully emotional instant that is lacking in the pro-
saic proverb.

The Finnish rune song also can take advantage of the union of a
nature image with an emotional expression, usually, however, in
reverse order.[10]

> My father discarded me,
> Like a crooked ax handle;
> My good mother forgot me,
> Like a sprung distaff;
> My little sister slipped by me,
> Like the squirrel on a dry tree;
> And my best brother shunned me,
> Like the fish the steep bank,
> Like the salmon the stony beach.

Usually an image of imagination in the rune song takes on a less
autonomous position than is the case with subjective imagery:

> See, others don their Sunday clothes,
> White clothes.

[10] This translation and the following ones are from Gustav Schmitt, *Deutsche
Rundschan* (1923), pp. 84–86.

> I wear only the dark clothes,
> Black clothes, mourning clothes.
>
> The women in the village then asked,
> "Why do you wear dark clothes?"
> "I wear dark clothes
> Because it is black in my heart."

An intense emotion can also be totally absent in an image, as is the case with the following rune song:

> Sing, sing, poor tongue,
> Speak and make known my sorrow, mouth!
> You will sing no songs
> And announce no joy
> When they lay you in the cold ground,
> In the frost-frozen ground,
> Board below, board above,
> And one to either side.

Besides heroic songs that presume a historical nucleus of actual events, lyric songs emanating from a pure source of inner emotion can represent the highest level attainable in folk poetry. Neither the epic nor lyric of every culture has attained this zenith. Very rarely have both reached the same height in a single nation.

In addition, every people has given international materials the unique stamp of its own character and culture, and a study of these is no less interesting than the elements common to all. Immigrant borrowings must first be determined according to their contents before native re-workings in the various countries can be compared and evaluated. After we have delineated the individual variants of the pattern of each area and from this insofar as possible the basic form, we can then, proceeding from the basic form, understand and explain the development of the local forms, and from these the formation of the individual variants.

XXI. Epilogue

IN A NEW SCIENCE it is not enough to be trained in method; one must also possess an independence of thought. The seeker for truth can trust no authority unconditionally, neither that of an individual mentor nor that of a general trend. Previously a young, progressive scholar had to suffer most seriously under the burden of traditional views. In our revolutionary era it is perhaps more difficult for him to free himself from seductive *new* theories in order to ensure the correct path for his work. In both cases he will be reproached by proponents of the prevailing movements, and with his divergent ideas he will stand alone and find little approval.

In this situation the scientific researcher can find comfort in the fact that a vote cannot be taken to decide scientific truth, that it existed before it was recognized and expressed, and that it remains even if all its professors disavow it. A scholar who has discovered a truth is initially its sole possessor. If his discovery leads to a reversal of previous views, he usually has to stand alone behind it for a time and fight for it. Recognition of it will come sooner or later but may remain elusive during his own lifetime, as was the case with the founder of the methodology presented here. The real seeker after truth may be confident, however, that if he has found a path leading to his goal, he will remain correct, even if he enjoys no followers whatever; and if, on the other hand, he has stumbled onto the wrong path, the approbation of the whole world would not have helped him to his goal.

The greatest danger and temptation for the researcher on an untrodden path, however, lies in the all-too-great reliance on the infallibility of his own techniques of interpretation. In themselves they may well be correct, but may still be applied by the researcher to cases where they are not appropriate. Of course he can still succeed in discovering a makeshift theory and thereby apparently save himself. A proponent of a science may not, however, function as a champion; he is also obliged to weigh his own views as an impartial judge. If he comes up against actualities, he should not adulterate them, but rather turn back and seek another way. If a researcher under the compulsion of his own knowledge or external, authoritative assertions decides to relinquish a philosophy that he has grown fond of, then the acid test of science has prevailed. Later it often becomes clear to him that that which seemed to be an obstacle has in fact led him to a new path that then led him further as well as rewarding him with even greater vistas.

For the scholar this sense of reality is no less important than what is called creativity. In the area of folk literature and folk belief beautiful castles in the air have been built with endlessly precious subtlety and fantasy on a foundation of insufficient, disordered, and unreliable materials—some even arbitrarily constructed. Many a scholar has convincingly depicted the folk fantasy as lively as his own. It is time to pass over from philosophizing and mythologizing to actual interpretation and microscopic study of available materials in order to be able to draw tenable, general conclusions corresponding to the facts from individual results.

Folklore criticism too must turn ever more to individual cases. General and formulaic criticism requires our knowledge to a minimal degree, quite apart from the fact that the excellence of one's own accomplishments and the severity of other scholars' judgment frequently stand in an inverse relationship to each other. Far more convincing than negative criticism is the positive solution of the same problem in another direction.

In our new, still relatively undeveloped science a young researcher who does not fear work and precision can, with an open eye and methodical procedures, bring to light many new discoveries. An awareness of this should stimulate him and give him satisfaction in the inescapable detail that requires, in all sciences, concentration to the extreme, constancy in minutia, and above all an incorruptible love of truth.

The results of a scientific labor can be infinitesimally small and yet of great methodological significance. The untying of a single knot can bring with it the unraveling of the whole snarl. A geographic study of apparently insignificant lullabies that are represented by so many variants in West Finland established and explained the migration of West Finnish heroic songs to East Finland and beyond the Finnish border, where they were preserved and discovered. It is no more necessary to suggest the value, in a national literary respect, that the analytic treatment of each line of Finnish heroic songs—in order to determine its original word-for-word form—has had than it is to establish the significance for world literature of the detailed reconstruction of the original content of some international Märchen.

Even the methodical treatment of relatively simple folk traditions will be no less useful as preparatory training for complicated studies of comparative literary history. Above all, work with folklore materials has brought the educated collector and scholar closer to the people and has led him to an understanding and love not only for his own people but also for mankind in general, in its lowest levels and most distant past.

Index